In this endlessly inspiring book, renowned textile and mixed-media artist Shelley Rhodes explains how she deconstructs and reassembles cloth, paper and other materials to create new pieces, often incorporating found objects and items she has collected over the years to add depth and emotional resonance.

She shows how to distress and manipulate fabric and alter surfaces using a wealth of exciting techniques, from piercing and devoré to rust-dyeing, soaking and even burying in a compost heap, and how larger pieces of work can be fragmented and the components worked on individually to form a series of smaller works with strong visual impact. There is also advice on exquisite ways to present and display your work, taking inspiration from museum collections and sixteenth-century cabinets of curiosities.

As well as stitching, special attention is given to darning and patching, traditionally seen simply as ways to prolong the life of garments but now appreciated as meaningful and decorative techniques in their own right, but Shelley also explores other wonderful ways to connect fabric and paper, bringing in materials like pins, tape, adhesive and plaster. The Japanese concepts of *wabi-sabi* – finding beauty in imperfection – and *mottainai* – using every last scrap – are also investigated, both of which constantly inform her work.

Beautifully illustrated with Shelley's own pieces alongside those of other leading artists, this fascinating book is the ideal companion for any textile artist wanting to bring notions of fragility and fragmentation, connection and repair into their own work.

Fragmentation and Repair

for Mixed-Media and Textile Artists

Shelley Rhodes

BATSFORD

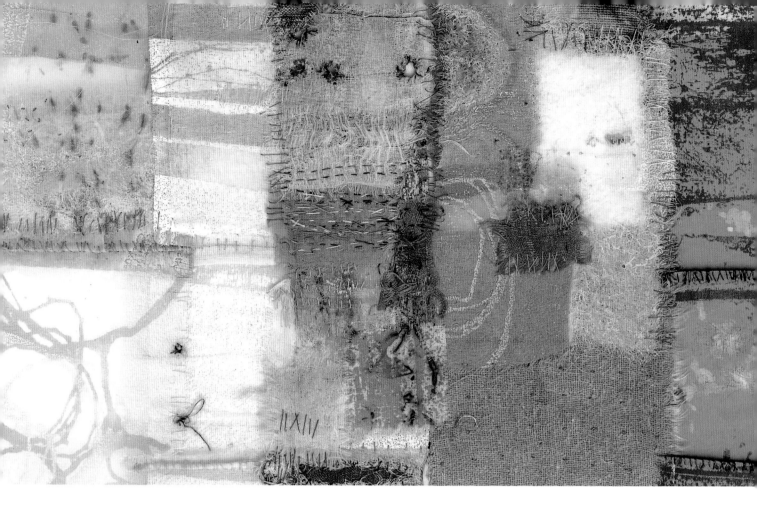

First published in the United Kingdom in 2021 by
Batsford
43 Great Ormond Street
London
WC1N 3HZ

ISBN 978-1-84994-610-0

A CIP catalogue record for this book is available from the British Library.

10 9 8 7 6 5 4 3 2

Reproduction by Rival Colour Ltd, UK
Printed and bound by Toppan Leefung, China

Title page Shelley Rhodes,
Weekly Stitch Practice.
5 x 12cm (2 x 4¾in) each.

Above Shelley Rhodes,
In Decline (detail).

Opposite Shelley Rhodes,
Little By Little (detail).

CONTENTS

INTRODUCTION

Fragmentation lies at the heart of my work. This book explores how I fragment and deconstruct cloth, paper and objects, before repairing and reassembling to make a new whole. It shows how fragments of found objects can inspire new work, as well as becoming part of the finished piece – perfect if you are a compulsive collector like me. Much of my work involves recycling materials while embracing the concept of *wabi-sabi*, the Japanese aesthetic that finds beauty in imperfection and impermanence. I am drawn to crumbling, stained, weathered surfaces and I show how natural processes can change the appearance and structure of materials, and how these can be replicated in a controlled way.

I refer to historical examples of Japanese *boro* and kantha, a technique that originated in Bangladesh and West Bengal, showing how tiny fragments of precious cotton were used to patch and repair worn out, distressed fabric to create a new layered, densely stitched cloth. I investigate ideas of repair and reconstruction, not only using stitch but introducing other materials and techniques too. I also demonstrate how previously completed work can be reworked.

I explore the power of multiples and how working in series can enhance the impact of individual pieces. I show how museum displays can be used to inspire content and presentation of work. Finally, I investigate the Japanese concept of *mottainai*, meaning to use every last scrap, as I demonstrate how tiny fragments can be used in collage and assemblage as well as becoming small works of art in their own right.

Above Shelley Rhodes, *Stitched Grid.* 12 x 46cm (4¾ x 18¼in).

Opposite Shelley Rhodes, *Coral Semblance.* 15 x 10cm (6 x 4in) each.

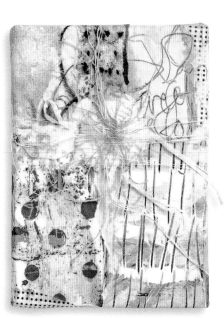

I share techniques of fragmentation and repair that I and other artists use in textile and mixed-media work. As always, I keep a record of my ideas, the progress made and notes regarding technique in workbooks, notebooks, sketchbooks or journals, and encourage you to do the same. (For further ideas about working in this way, refer to my first book, *Sketchbook Explorations*.) I have included examples of techniques that I use, with some suggestions that I hope you will try.

HISTORICAL FRAGMENTS

For centuries, piecing, patching and repairing cloth were a necessity for many different cultures. Ancient fragments of cloth up to 12,000 years old have been discovered in countries such as Egypt, China and Peru. In Europe, layers of quilted fabric, thought to have been used as part of a soldier's armour for warmth and protection, have been found dating back to the early Middle Ages. One of the earliest surviving complete patchworks is a coverlet dating from 1718.

Quilting

Quilting is a method of stitching layers of material together – usually two layers of fabric with padding or wadding in between. Quilts can be created using whole pieces of cloth but in this book my focus is on quilts that use piecing and patching for the top layer. Many pieced quilts are joined in regular, geometric patterns, or from patchwork blocks made using a paper template and stitched together in a grid format. However, pieced quilts can be bold and free-form, like the quilts of Gee's Bend, Alabama. My work tends to be influenced by less formal methods of patching and piecing cloth, such as Japanese *boro* (see page 12).

Not all patchwork is quilted. *Jogakbo* is a style of Korean patchwork traditionally used to make wrapping cloths (known as *bojagi*). Geometric-shaped scraps are sewn together in an irregular, improvised way, using a special seaming technique to create a flat seam, which gives the cloth the appearance of a stained-glass window.

Below Patched and stitched cloth details.

Opposite Traditional kantha, made in East Bengal, c. 1885. Embroiderers' Guild Collection.

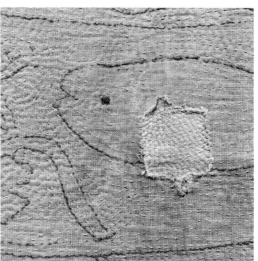

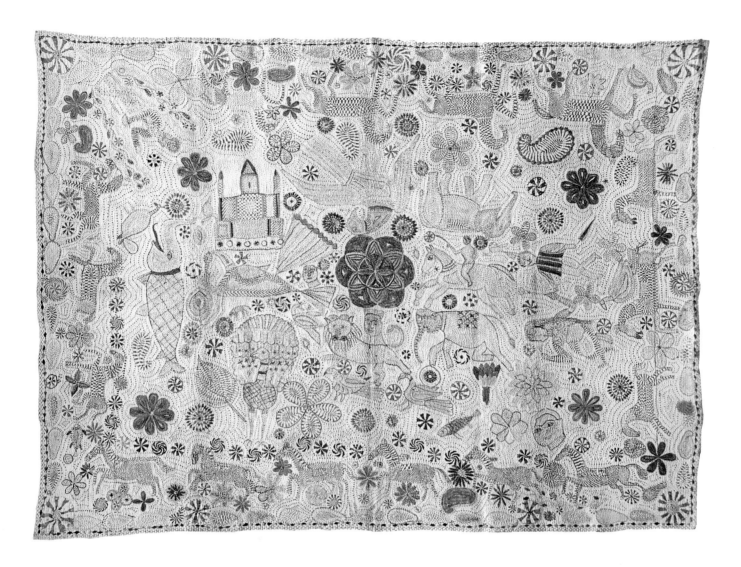

KANTHA

The word 'kantha' is derived from Sanskrit, denoting a rag or patched garment. They are double-sided embroideries created from worn-out saris and dhotis, made in the Bengal region of the Indian subcontinent. It is unclear when the making of kantha first began: the earliest mention in literature dates from 500 years ago, but the oldest surviving examples originate from the early nineteenth century. Recycling, repurposing and the stitching of layers of cloth together lie at the heart of traditional kantha making. Traditionally, white saris with coloured borders were worn, and when these became old and threadbare, the long pieces of fine cotton cloth were folded into three or four layers and held together with running stitch.

Some traditional kanthas are richly embroidered with scenes and domestic objects from everyday life. Others depict whimsical figures and quirky animals and birds, or have more abstract geometric shapes, or floral and leaf motifs. These motifs are 'drawn' with running stitch, using a thread that contrasts in colour, and then filled in with decorative patterns. In old kanthas, the coloured threads were sometimes withdrawn from the border patterns woven on the edges of the saris. Other stitches besides running stitch were also used for the filling stitches, such as back stitch and stem stitch; the placement and density of the stitches affects the texture of the cloth, causing a rippling on the surface. Traditionally, kanthas were made by women and used for household items such as bed quilts and for swaddling babies, as the cloth was usually soft, warm and comforting.

Today, recycling and repurposing continues, using coloured and printed saris in which fragments are pieced and patched together in layers. Multiple rows of running stitch unify and hold the layers in place. There are many stitch co-operatives run on a commercial basis, some creating exciting contemporary twists on traditional techniques, and although the pieces they make are not traditional kanthas, they are still referred to as kantha.

Below Shelley Rhodes, *Not Quite Kantha*. Kantha techniques combined with collage, plaster and clay slip. 27 x 31cm (10¾ x 12¼in).

Above Contemporary cloths using kantha techniques (details).

Opposite Dorothy Tucker, *Plates and Leaves*. 33 x 109cm (13 x 43in).

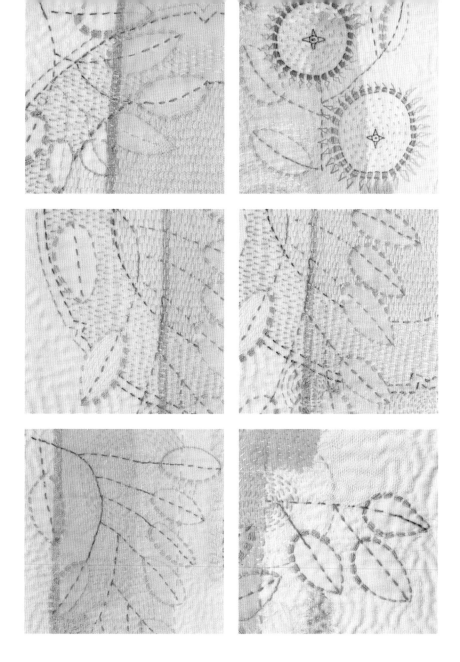

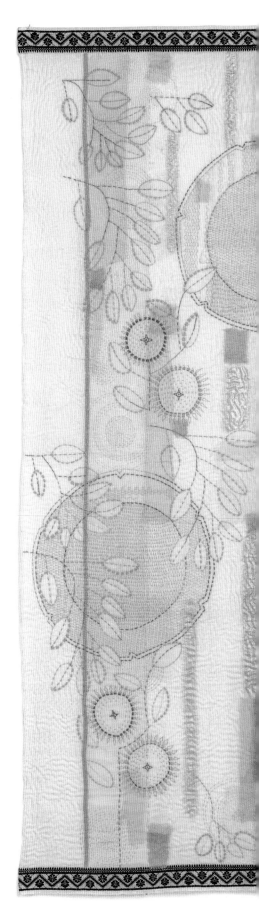

Dorothy Tucker's stitched work draws on traditional ways of making kantha. *Plates and Leaves* is made from a fine cotton sari, folded into four layers. The length of the piece and the inclusion of the woven borders reference the sari from which it was made. She explains:

'A vertical grey line, just visible under the top layer, makes use of a stripe woven into the sari end. Stripes like these, which often feature on old traditional kantha, inspired me to insert strips of coloured cotton underneath the top layer and also to add patches of colour on top. Once the fabrics have been positioned, the layers are secured with lines of even running stitch. Domestic objects are often depicted on traditional kantha, which led me to use plates and leaves on this piece. All the motifs are outlined, then coloured and filled in with stitched patterns. Finally, all the remaining spaces are quilted.'

Not quite kantha

I often think of my work in terms of being 'not quite kantha', as I take the essence of kantha making but work in an inventive, experimental way in order to make contemporary pieces. All samples seen here are made from at least three layers, held together using simple repetitive stitch, and examples 2–5 introduce a variety of non-traditional materials. Working small allows extensive experimentation and exploration before taking any ideas forward into larger pieces of work (see work on page 8).

Example 1 A traditional approach using lightweight layers of fine fabric joined with rows of running stitch.

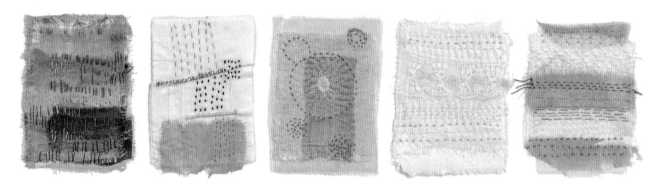

Example 2 Combining soft, lightweight fabric with other materials, including wool blanket, felt, paper and plastic.

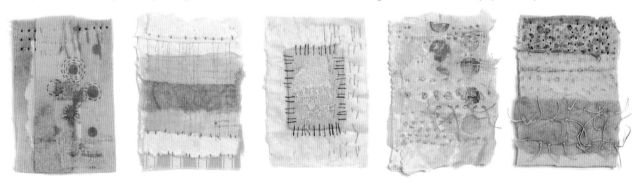

Example 3 Creating 'alternative stitches' by using fine wire, staples, twine, raffia or pins. Stitches do not have to run in straight lines. Layers are held together with knots, tied threads, couching or other decorative stitches.

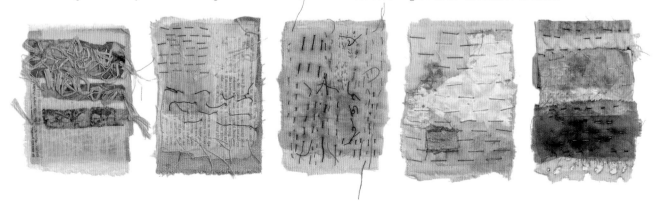

Example 4 Trapping fragments within the layers using natural or man-made objects, such as pressed leaves and flowers, tiny twigs, pebbles, sea glass, shells, rusty objects or plastic fragments. Flat objects work best; once stitched, metal items can be wetted and left to rust and stain the cloth.

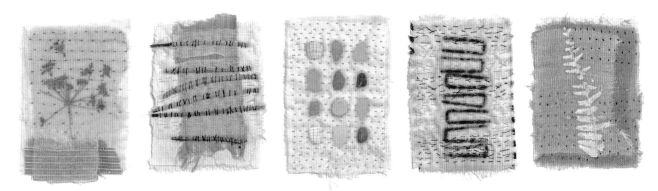

Example 5 Coating the stitched fabric with media such as paint, plaster, gesso, clay slip and wax. Samples can be cracked, scratched and coloured, then restitched.

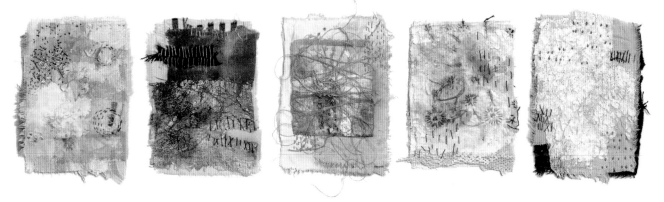

Below Shelley Rhodes, *In the Canyon* (detail), with layered cloth with running stitch inspired by kantha.

JAPANESE BORO

The term *boro* is derived from a Japanese word that translates as 'tattered, worn out, torn and crumbling' and describes heavily patched and repaired clothing and bedding made through necessity in the far north of Japan.

Boro garments were work clothes made and worn by families of poor fishermen and peasant farmers in the late nineteenth century in an area called Aomori, where winters are extremely harsh. Essentially made from rags, repaired and patched with many layers stitched together, these utilitarian garments were also altered and reassembled into bed covers, with one item utilized to repair another. Fabric scraps were used to patch holes and thin areas, which was repeated again and again, increasing the layers and adding greater strength to the material.

In the north of Japan, clothing was usually made from hemp, which is rough and scratchy and cold in winter, so layers were stitched together and sometimes padded with hemp fuzz to add insulation, like a form of wadding. Further south, towards what is now Tokyo and Kyoto, farmers wore cotton, but the Aomori region was too cold to grow cotton, and only a small quantity of this material found its way north, usually via seafaring traders, until the railway line was opened at the end of the nineteenth century. As a result, cotton fabric was rare and expensive, so the tiniest snippets were saved as they were very precious and valuable. Cloth was handed down from one generation to the next, and young girls would have tiny scraps of cloth as a dowry to take with them when they married.

Above left Japanese *boro yogi* sleeping garment, shaped like a giant kimono, late 1800s to early 1900s.

Above right Japanese *boro* patchwork futon cover with sashiko stitching, late 1800s to early 1900s.

Opposite Japanese *boro* repairs (details).

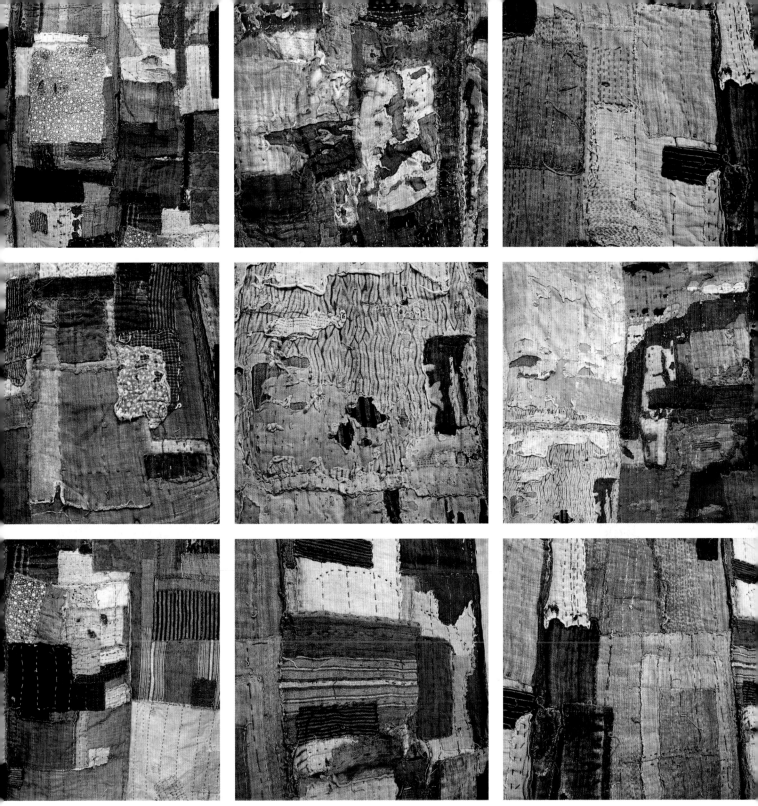

Until relatively recently, *boro* was regarded as a sign of poverty and therefore seen as shameful. It was not until the mid-twentieth century that these garments, futon covers and patched cloths were collected and preserved, largely through the efforts of Chuzaburo Tanaka, who recognized their importance as items of historical and cultural significance. He brought *boro* textiles to the world's attention by setting up and displaying his collection in the Amuse Museum in Tokyo (now sadly closed); I was allowed to handle items in the collection when I visited the museum and some of the garments are extremely heavy due to many layers being stitched together.

Cotton sakabukuro sake bags

During the nineteenth and early twentieth centuries, Japanese sake brewers used cloth bags, known as *sakabukuro*, to filter sediment from unrefined sake; the bags were filled then hung, allowing refined sake to drip out into collection vats. Every summer, fermented persimmon juice was applied to the bags to strengthen them and infuse them with antibacterial properties. They became stained and variegated until they almost resembled brown leather. If the bags became damaged, they were carefully patched and hand stitched using thick cotton threads to extend their life. These essential repairs are a wonderful example of *wabi-sabi* (see Discarded and Abandoned, page 16).

These traditional practices have influenced my own work as I employ methods of repairing, piecing, patching and staining. I always keep the smallest leftover scraps and have bags of tiny fragments saved to reuse. Working this way allows flexibility, as sections can be cut, moved and restitched. If I am unhappy with an area, I can simply cut and reassemble, or cover it with a patch of fabric. Small sections can be worked before joining to become a larger piece, making work portable and always close to hand when I have time free, however short.

Above Japanese *sakabukuro* (cotton sake bag), early to mid-1900s.

Below Shelley Rhodes, *Kantha Fragments* (details).

Opposite Shelley Rhodes, *Marked* (detail). Hanging with patches and repairs. 210 x 78cm (82¾ x 30¾in).

 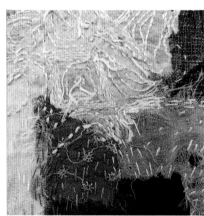 

DISCARDED AND ABANDONED

I am drawn to things that have been discarded, lost, left behind or abandoned. This could be on the coast, in the countryside or in an urban setting. I look closely, constantly observing, recording and collecting, as I seek out broken, mundane, neglected and overlooked things.

WABI-SABI

Finding beauty in imperfection and impermanence is the aesthetic behind the Japanese concept of *wabi-sabi*. It is about encompassing natural decay and ageing, and appreciating something that is weathered and showing signs of patina, rather than an item that is shiny and new. It could be something that is fragmented or uneven; it may be a piece that has been repaired, but showing and rejoicing in the repair, rather than trying to hide or disguise it. It is about noticing and reacting to small details rather than grand gestures. It is also about being less materialistic, reusing the things we already have by mending, recycling and reinventing. It is transient and ever-changing, sometimes unfinished and incomplete, but often quiet, minimal, calm and uncluttered.

Many of these ideas have an influence on my work. Most of the fabric I use is repurposed and recycled, such as bed linen, tablecloths, handkerchiefs, curtains and garments. I like the soft, worn quality of well-used fabric, which may include small holes, marks and stains. Colours are usually slightly faded and gentler than they would once have been. Sometimes, I unpick the seams to reveal how the fabric would have looked before repeated washing, handling and general wear and tear. This recycling also has a positive impact on the environment.

I photograph examples of *wabi-sabi* to use as inspiration for drawing and mark-making, or for extracting a colour palette. I am drawn to crumbling, derelict buildings, to cracked plaster and peeling paint that reveals layers of colours beneath the surface; to painted metal that has been weathered and distressed over time, perhaps affected by salty seawater. Looking closely reveals amazing colours and beautiful marks that are often perfect in their imperfection.

'Being creative is seeing the same thing as everybody else but thinking of something different.'

Albert Einstein

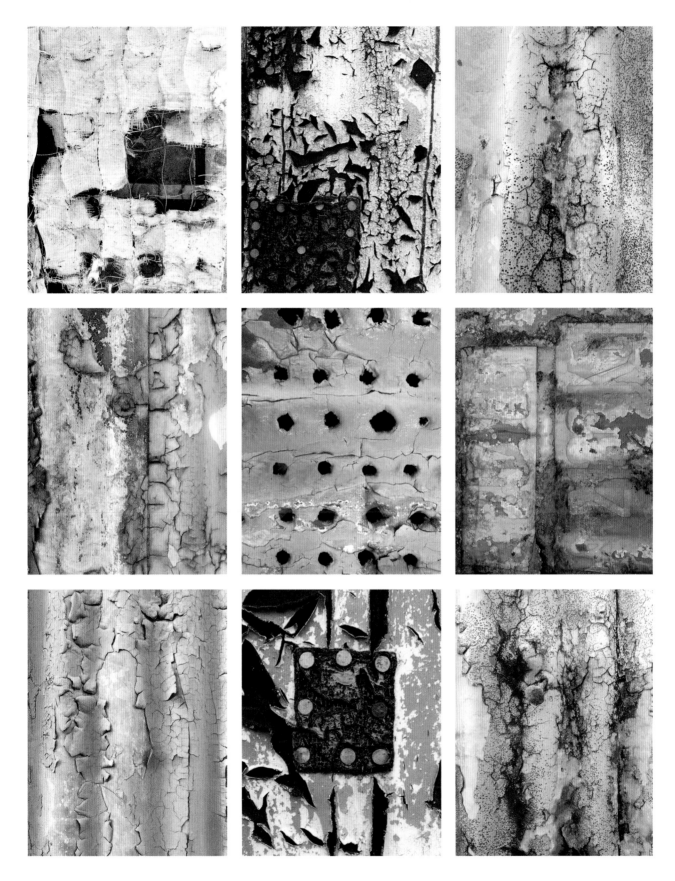

Wabi-sabi photographs.

Backstreets is a series of mixed-media work exploring surface texture, inspired by the crumbling buildings I photographed while visiting Cuba. Cloth was fragmented, manipulated and stitched, then coated with layers of paint, plaster and clay slip, partially embedding the stitches (see Mixed Media, page 132). Fragments were joined and further stitched marks made before they were collaged onto boards. Colour was applied with layers of ink, pigment, oil and wax, before scratching, nailing and wrapping.

Left Shelley Rhodes, *Backstreets Series*.
Mixed media on MDF.
33 x 15cm (13 x 6in).

Opposite Shelley Rhodes, *Corrugated Series II*.
Mixed media incorporating found metal.
40 x 29cm (15¾ x 11½in).

Below Corrugated iron photographs.

For many years, I have been drawn to weathered corrugated iron. The sheets are often pieced together like a giant patchwork of metal – joined with rivets, screws, nails and wire. Sometimes they have been painted, then over time the paint peels and flakes, allowing areas of rust to emerge. I made a series of work inspired by these panels, where the linear ridges of metal were weathered and distressed over time, the paint scratched, flaking and pitted with rust marks. The colours that I used were inspired by the painted metal sheets. Fabric was dyed, painted and screen printed before being fragmented and reassembled in response to the patches of corrugated iron. Small items of rusty metal found on location became part of these mixed-media collages.

RECYCLE, REUSE

Using any material that has had a previous life adds layers of history and interest to work. I seek out used papers and fabric. Favourite papers include old ledger pages with handwritten text created with dip pens; pages from discarded books that have turned yellow, with folded corners and scribbled pencil notes; or grids and charts stamped with numbers and seemingly random ticks and crosses. I enjoy seeing glimpses of text showing through when the paper is partially painted or printed.

I use very little new fabric in my work, choosing instead to recycle pre-used cloth. It has a very different quality and character to a new piece of fabric. It is often soft to the touch, through years of handling and washing; imperfections, colour variations, marks, stains and holes add further layers of intrigue and interest. There is something very beautiful and delicate about worn, threadbare cloth – the fragile, semi-transparent fabric is lovely for layering as it allows glimpses of the underlying fabric to show through.

I recycle my clothes and household linens, gather from charity shops, and search for discarded scraps of cloth while beachcombing. If these rescued materials are distressed, stained and threadbare, they need very little intervention from me. However, there are ways to encourage and speed up the process (see Altering Surfaces, page 24).

'I only see the faults, flaws, the imperfections. That attracts me.'

Yohji Yamamoto

Rescued materials.

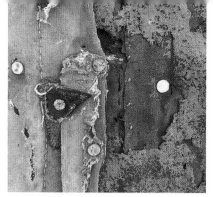  

SALVAGED

Over the centuries, many artists have salvaged redundant materials to use in their work. Robert Rauschenberg made a series called *Combines*, in which he assembled and combined discarded objects with collage and painting. In Australia, Rosalie Gascoigne gathered weathered materials, such as abandoned road signs, wooden drink crates, corrugated iron panels and cable reel ends, to fragment then reconstruct. When I saw her piece *High Country*, I was struck by the power of the simple construction, consisting of 16 carefully arranged squares of painted corrugated iron panels.

I often use stuff that would otherwise be scrapped, searching for abandoned materials that have survived against the odds. For my series *Found*, I used discarded parquet floor rescued from a skip. Stitched fragments of fabric were nailed and wrapped around the wooden blocks. The pieces were made in response to sheds made from overturned, recycled herring boats on the island of Lindisfarne, in north-east England. Their tattered tarpaulin is nailed down but exposed to the elements, and the scraps tend to flap around in the wind.

'You begin with the possibilities of the material.'

Robert Rauschenberg

Top Lindisfarne boat shed photographs.

Above Shelley Rhodes, *Found*.
Recycled parquet floor blocks.
28 x 7cm (11 x 2¾in) each.

El Anatsui is a Ghanaian artist who uses everyday salvaged materials. He is renowned for using multiple small fragments of scrap metal in his work, such as tin cans, metal seals and bottle tops. In his piece *Bleeding Takari II*, he flattens the metal seals from African liquor bottles, then cuts the metal into strips, before sewing them together with copper wire to create a monumental draping, fabric-like installation. Inspired by his work, I rescued the little metal pieces from old floppy discs that were being thrown away. Some had squares cut into them, reminding me of frames or slide mounts. I cut, folded, hammered, scratched and sanded the metal, then used them to frame fragments of sea glass and other beachcombing finds. These were mounted and stitched onto small collages, made with drawings, text and marks inspired by my coastal collection.

Shelley Rhodes,
Coastal Fragments.
Salvaged frames with
found fragments.
5 x 3cm (2 x 1¼in) each.

ALTERING
SURFACES

The transformation of surfaces is an important aspect of my work. There are many ways to do this and I have investigated a variety of methods, as outlined in this chapter.

MANIPULATION

Paper changes with manipulation and continually handling it can alter its surface. *Momigami* is the Japanese art of paper kneading, which involves the repeated scrunching, crumpling and unfolding of paper. This manipulation softens the paper and it takes on a more fabric-like quality. If paper is quite stiff to start with, it helps to spray it lightly with a mist of water, or use a little oil on your hands. The edges tend to be particularly vulnerable when you first begin, so start very gently and try folding the corners in to protect them.

Some types of paper are easier to manipulate than others and this will depend on many things: for example, what the paper is made from, the length of fibres used and the finish. It is interesting to explore a range of different papers to see what works best for your needs. Fabric can also be softened through rubbing and manipulation, but to a lesser extent.

Shelley Rhodes, *Marks of Time* (details).

'Play is the highest form of research.'

Albert Einstein

Above Weathered sample.

Right Shelley Rhodes, *Weathered*.
Paper left in garden, bonded and stitched.
56 x 17cm (22 x 6¾in) each.

WEATHERING

Physical decay, weathering and wear and tear make some things more visually appealing. The colour, texture and patina of cloth, paper, metal and wood can be transformed in a dynamic and exciting way. Many changes are transient and occur slowly, continually altering over a period of time and creating imperfections that can often look beautiful.

Paper and fabric can simply be left outside, exposing them to the elements. A piece of paper placed under a shrub will be gently nibbled over time by garden creatures, making small incremental changes and creating a beautiful lacy effect. I bonded fragments of weathered and nibbled paper to cotton organdie before machine stitching, then leaving it outside again.

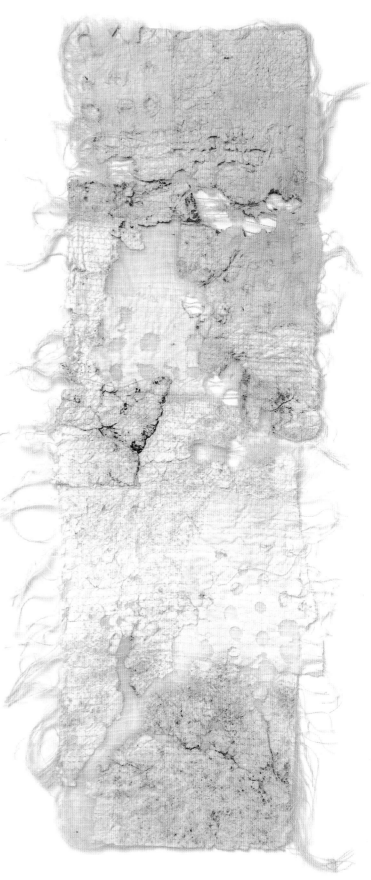

If a grid is stitched onto paper, a delicate fragmented mesh can be made by wetting it then gently rubbing some of the paper away; or it can be left outside to break down naturally over time. Experiment by using different types of paper – strong serviettes work well. Lightweight cloth can be treated in the same way. A similar grid can be made by using polyester thread on cotton fabric, then partially applying devoré paste (see Devoré, page 38). This will remove areas of the cotton, leaving a fragmented grid. Once the delicate mesh has been created, it can be dipped and coated with paint, plaster, ceramic slip or wax (see Mixed Media, page 132). I used these fragile grid structures to represent broken coral in *Only Five Percent*.

Top Mesh grid samples coated with different media.

Above Shelley Rhodes, *Only Five Percent*. Four pieces each about 23 x 13cm (9 x 5in).

Right Shelley Rhodes, *Marks of Time VI.*
100 x 23cm (39¼ x 9in).

Below *Marks of Time Series* (details).

A piece of fabric hung on a washing line will fade and soften in the wind, sun and rain. Compare the difference, leaving it for a month, six months or a year. I did this when making a series called *Marks of Time.* The work combined small fragments of printed and marked paper and fabric. Cellulose paste was used to hold all the fragments in place on a cotton ground. The paste was applied liberally then left to dry on a sheet of plastic. Once dry, the whole thing peeled off easily. I stitched into it using machine and hand stitching. It felt quite stiff and there was a slight shine due to the paste, so I hung it on the washing line to weather. It softened and changed over time. After several weeks, some areas began to fall apart slightly. I checked it periodically and made ongoing stitched repairs. I altered it further by gently manipulating some areas and lightly sanding others. The work developed slowly over several months.

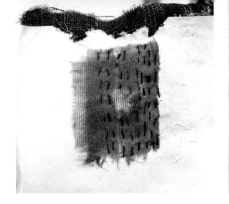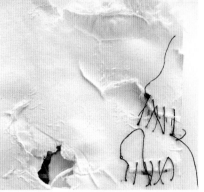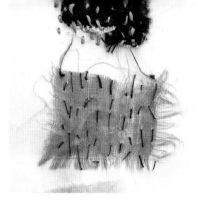

WASHING

The repeated washing or boiling of fabric softens it and fades the colour. It encourages edges to fray and holes to increase in size. Cut a piece of fabric into two and observe the changes by washing one half every time you use the washing machine. Compare it to the original, unwashed half after 20, 50 or 100 washes. I washed one piece of work 100 times to see how it compared to an unwashed piece.

Paper can be washed with care. I placed a small sketchbook inside a net lingerie wash bag for protection then washed it on a regular cycle; when I opened the bag, the sketchbook had virtually disintegrated into a ball of mushed paper! I tried a second book, containing heavier-weight paper, on a short, low-temperature setting. The wet pages became slightly creased, torn and distressed, with random holes and tears. I repaired these using stitch, staples, tape, metal fragments, patched fabric and wire – creating a little book of experimental repairs.

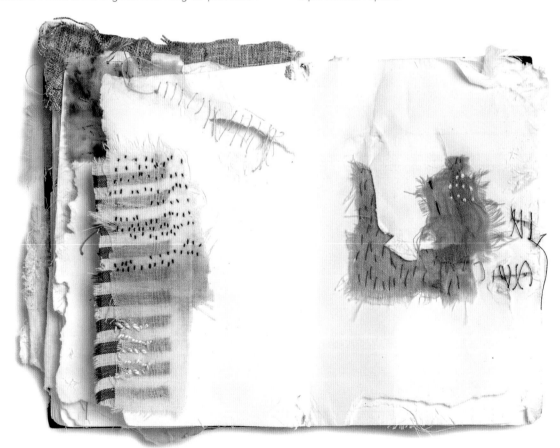

Top, this page and opposite *Repaired Sketchbook* (details).

Above Shelley Rhodes, *Repaired Sketchbook*.
11 x 15cm (4¼ x 6in).

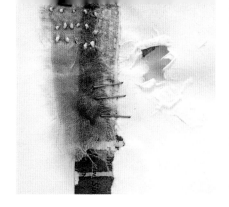 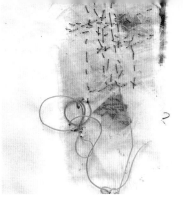 

SOAKING

Soaking cloth or paper will alter it. Soaking in seawater affects rusty metal and accelerates the staining of cloth. Debbie Lyddon has perfected a technique in which fabric is soaked in salt water, using a solution she mixes herself: the water is left to evaporate, allowing salt crystals to form on the cloth.

'Each salt work is left to soak in a shallow bath of salt water. The water is allowed to evaporate naturally – a process that can take up to three months – as the water evaporates salt crystals form. Salt is a corrosive material and so the work is expected to degenerate very slowly over time.'

Below Debbie Lyddon,
Exposed: Enclosed (detail).

BURYING

Burying cloth in the garden not only stains and discolours it but also starts the process of disintegration, allowing natural fabric to break down. Fashion designer Hussein Chalayan buried his entire graduation show collection next to iron filings to create rusted, partially decomposed garments. Buried items need to be checked periodically to assess the changes. I set up an experiment by making a series of four similar fabric collages. I buried three in the compost heap so I could explore the deterioration over different periods of time by comparing them to the fourth (unburied) collage. My plan was to leave one for three months, one for six months and one for nine months. However, when I retrieved them after three months, they had virtually disappeared. I managed to salvage one that was partially destroyed. They obviously did not need to be left for so long, particularly over the wet winter months.

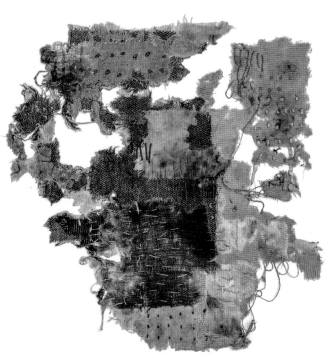

Shelley Rhodes, *Buried Samples* (before and after).
17 x 16cm (6¾ x 6¼in) each.

ABRASION

Paper and fabric can be softened through abrasion. Rubbing and handling will change the surface quality (see Manipulation, page 24). Surfaces can be altered using sandpaper or wet-and-dry paper, and this technique is particularly effective when the surface being abraded is placed on an uneven rock or stone. The repetitive motion of a felting needle on fabric can alter and distress the surface, which can be done by hand or by using an embellisher machine. Different fabrics break down at different rates, depending on the weave and density. A small cut hole can help to start the process before the barbed needles fray and soften the edges. Alternatively, a wire brush will work in a similar way. These are often sold in sets of three from hardware stores – one soft, one mid-strength and one with very stiff wire, which is much more abrasive. The soft one is good to use on paper or for gently softening the edges of fabric, but be careful to protect your work surfaces by working on an old wooden chopping board.

STAINING

Cloth can be wrapped around various objects, then left to create stains and marks. Wrapping cloth around rusty objects combined with foliage, leaves, berries and organic kitchen waste can produce some dramatic results.

The simplest method is to wrap cloth around rusty metal objects and leave outdoors for days, weeks or even months, allowing rainwater to soak the bundle, colouring and staining the surface.

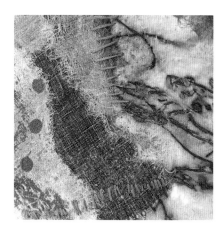 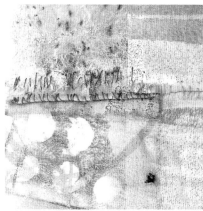 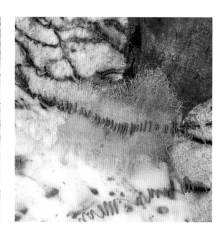

In order to get prints and marks from leaves, flowers and vegetation, they need to be wrapped in bundles and then boiled for at least an hour. Eco printing and dyeing is a complex subject and there are many specialist books and workshops that will demonstrate advanced techniques, but there is a very simple method that I find to be effective. Place foliage onto strips of fabric and paper, then roll tightly around a slightly rusty, discarded tin can. The tin-can bundle then needs to be boiled for an hour or two in a dedicated vessel that will not be used for food: I use a rusty old wok, which probably affects the outcome, perhaps making the prints slightly darker than they would have been if I had used an aluminium pot. Sometimes I add used teabags, coffee grounds or onion skins to the boiling water. This type of staining, colouring and mark-making can be carefully recorded and adjusted, as many variables will affect the results. However, there is a certain amount of serendipity and unpredictability that I enjoy; I know that I will be selecting, cutting and fragmenting the stained pieces, so I do not worry about trying to achieve pleasing marks over the whole piece.

Above Rust-marked fabric (details).

Below Bundles wrapped around tin cans.

Prior to staining, I often join different types of fabric and paper, using a combination of hand and machine stitching, as I like it when prints and marks work across different grounds, becoming embedded in the stitched surface. I use recycled fabrics and papers (book pages or recycled drawings, for example) as small areas will often show through the new prints. Once they have been dyed, I select areas to cut or tear before rearranging to make a new composition. Stitch is used to join and to create further marks for embellishment.

'One of the advantages of being disorderly is that one is constantly making exciting discoveries.'

A. A. Milne

Left Eco-dyed paper and fabric.

Below Shelley Rhodes, *Lockdown Marks.* Fragmented eco prints, reassembled and stitched. 10 x 87cm (4 x 34¼in) and 8 x 87cm (3¼ x 34¼in). Details shown opposite.

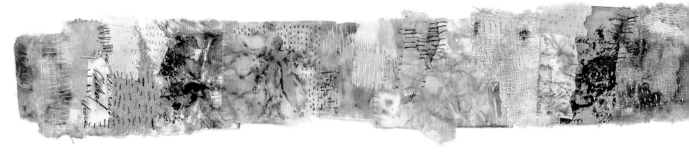

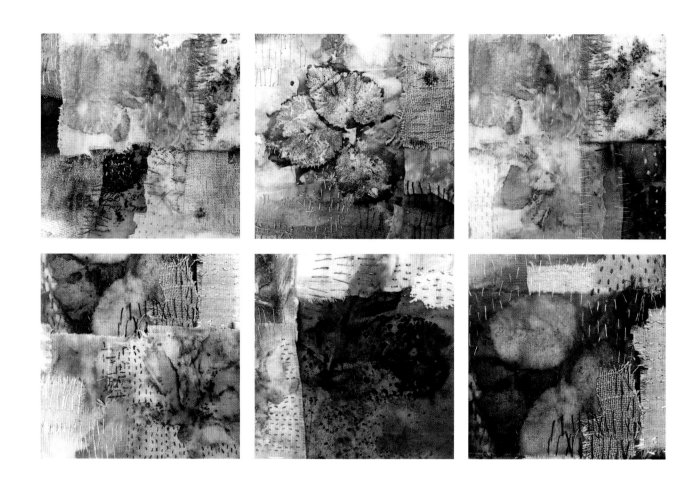

Alice Fox made a variety of work in which she used the reactive potential of found metal combined with a wetting agent to stain the fibres she had attached to it, as she explains:

'Tide Line *is a series of small woven surfaces in which rusty metal objects gathered on beaches were embedded during the process of weaving. Each woven piece was repeatedly dipped in seawater, mimicking the repetition of the tide. Over a period of time the salt water "pulled" rust from the metal object and stained the woven structure organically, integrating the constructed soft element with the hard object.'*

Similarly, she used an oak gall dye bath to make *Lime Kiln Objects* (see Found Fragments, page 116). The strong tannins in the dye bath reacted with the iron oxide of the metal items to create an impressive range of stains and marks.

Above Alice Fox, *Tide Line.*

In both the *Tide Line* and *Lime Kiln Objects* series, she describes how

'… the staining amalgamates the new and old elements, combining the two into a whole new type of configuration. This kind of staining is relatively uncontrolled, and the results are unpredictable. This happenstance is important to me and I enjoy the process of setting things up, bringing different elements together and then seeing what develops.'

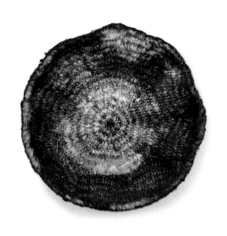

BURNING AND SCORCHING

Pieces can be burnt or scorched, but you must always do so outdoors with safety in mind: work on a fireproof surface – I use an old metal biscuit tin or baking tray and I have a bucket of water and water spray bottle nearby. Cloth and paper can be set alight then quickly extinguished to burn the edges. Dampening paper or cloth first enables a slower burn. Scorch marks can be made using a hot iron, or smoke marks created by holding damp work over a burning tealight or candle. Soot and ash can be used to make marks or be rubbed into surfaces. John Cage combined smoke, soot and watercolour to make a series of drawings, including a huge scroll called *New River Rocks and Smoke*, embracing the chance marks that smoke made on the dampened paper.

To explore how holes can be burnt using a soldering iron or incense stick, see Burning Holes, page 41.

Top Alice Fox, *Lime Kiln Objects*.

Left, above and below Burning samples.

MAKING HOLES

I like to work in layers, so I often consider removing as well as adding when making work. Taking away parts of the top surface reveals glimpses of colours and marks in the layers below, while making holes in a single layer opens a void, creating fragility while allowing light and shadows to become part of the work. There are many ways to make holes – by cutting, burning, punching, piercing and withdrawing threads.

WITHDRAWING THREADS

Debbie Lyddon is intrigued by holes not only as marks, but by how a hole defines or draws attention to a space; how they connect one side of a sculpture to another by directing vision. She often creates holes within her work, as well as withdrawing threads to reveal spaces, as she has done in *Shadow Pots*:

'Shadow Pots are inspired by the black-netted lobster pots that sit stacked outside my studio – they use a technique of removing the weft threads from cloth to create holes in cloth. Pierced into a piece of cloth, a hole lets light and air through and reveals what is behind. If the sun or another light source shines onto the pots, a shadow is revealed. The shadow becomes another work in its own right – a sort of ephemeral drawing that changes and moves as the light source interacts with the work.'

Right Debbie Lyddon, *Shadow Pots*. 78 x 14 x 8.5cm (30¾ x 5½ x 3¼in).

CUTTING HOLES

Fabric and paper can be hand cut using sharp scissors or a scalpel and cutting mat. Shapes can be completely cut out, or a small section can be left intact, allowing the cut area to be folded back – this could be left as a flap or held down in a variety of ways. Once holes have been cut, the edges can be softened or distressed using a small wire brush or old toothbrush. Similarly, washing fabric alters hard, cut edges, softening them as they become slightly frayed.

Laser cutting is a method of cutting holes, shapes and patterns into various materials, including fabric, paper, metal, wood and acrylic. Designs can be sent to specialist firms who will cut your designs out for you.

Holes can be cut or torn out of paper or card to make a stencil. Many pre-cut commercial stencils are available to buy and it is possible to use machines to cut your own stencil designs. Mylar sheets can be used in such machines but they can also be hand cut to make a long-lasting stencil. I tend to hand cut my stencils using a scalpel and cutting mat. Designing and cutting your own stencils makes any subsequent work unique and personal. The stencils can be used to add marks, patterns and colour to paper and fabric, and work particularly well when used with a gel printing plate.

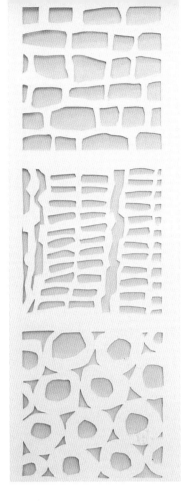

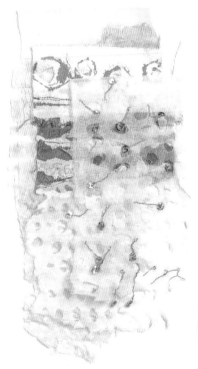
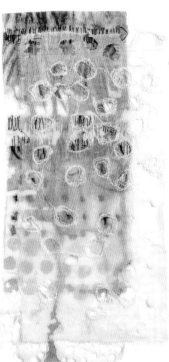
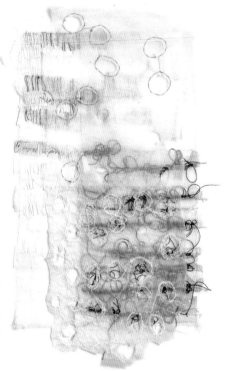

Top right Paper cut-outs.

Above Layered hole samples.

PIERCING AND PUNCHING

Hole punches can be used on paper or lightweight fabric. Sometimes I intentionally just bruise and mark the fabric, rather than making a clean hole. A Japanese screw punch, as used by bookbinders, allows single holes to be made anywhere – not just along edges. Fabric and paper can be pierced using a bradawl or needle. This can be done by hand and is easier if the surface is pulled taut in an embroidery hoop or pinned to a frame. Paper can be pierced by running it through a sewing machine without any thread in the needle (it makes raised holes, a bit like braille). Washes of colour can be applied, or chalks, pastels and pigments can be rubbed into the textured surface.

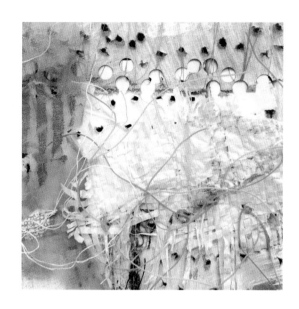

DEVORÉ

The process of devoré is also known as 'burn out'. Devoré paste will 'devour' or 'eat into' cellulose fibres such as cotton, linen, viscose and rayon, while leaving synthetic and protein fibres, such as silk, intact. It is usually used on viscose/silk velvet to remove only the pile in order to create a pattern. However, I like to use it to make holes in cotton fabric. Various pastes and gels can be purchased from specialist craft shops. Alternatively, it is possible to mix your own paste (see devoré paste recipe, page 41).

I made a series of work in response to the holes and marks observed on small fragments of coral. *Coral Cloths* were made using devoré paste (see Fragility, page 44). The paste can be painted, printed or stamped onto fabric, or it can be applied by using a silk screen, stencil or thermofax screen. When painting dots, I sometimes pin the cloth to a frame to stop it from spreading; at other times, I work directly on paper or a plastic sheet, allowing shapes to evolve as it touches the surface.

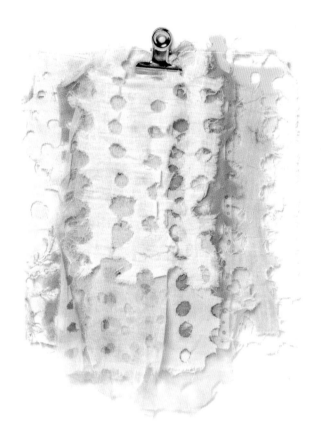

Top right Holes made by piercing and punching.

Right Fabric bundle with holes.

Opposite, above Shelley Rhodes, *Coral Cloth* (folded).

Opposite, below *Coral Cloths* (details).

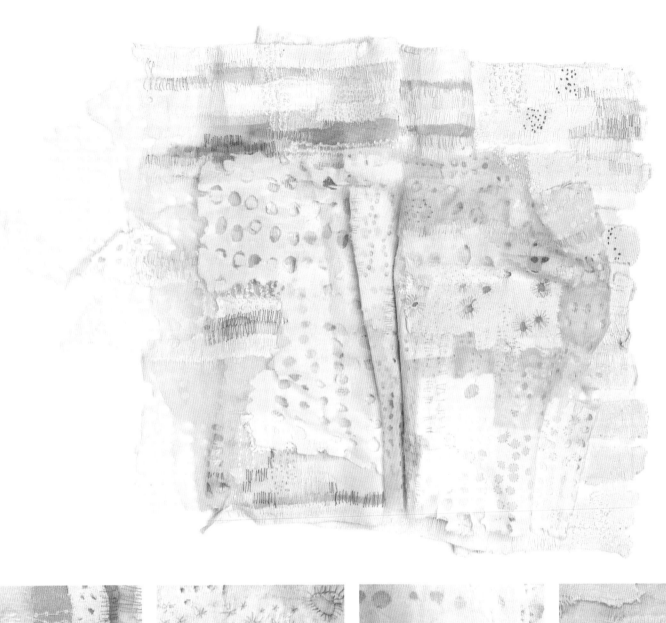

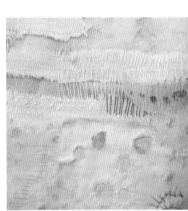

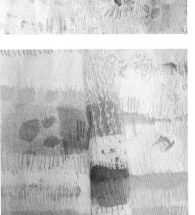
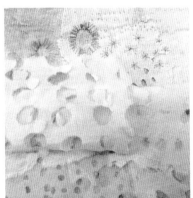
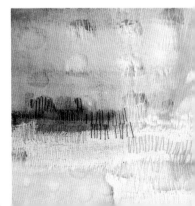

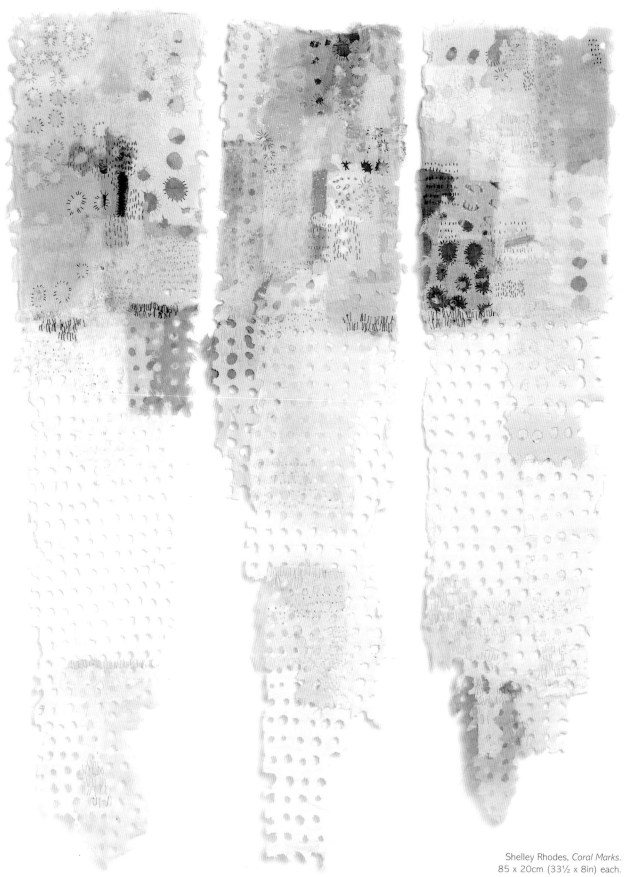

Devoré paste recipe

I mix small batches of the paste as it becomes less effective over time, although it is possible to freeze, then defrost and reuse when needed. I use a dedicated set of measuring spoons (never to be used for food preparation), and that way no weighing is required. Always wear a mask and gloves for protection when mixing and applying the paste.

Step 1 First mix Indalca paste (thickener), by adding one teaspoon of Indalca powder to four tablespoons of water. Use a mini whisk to mix the powder in rapidly to stop lumps from forming.

Step 2 In a separate container, mix one dessertspoon of aluminium sulphate into two tablespoons of water. Add five drops of glycerine and mix well.

Step 3 Whisk the aluminium sulphate/glycerine mix into the Indalca paste, combining the two.

Once the paste has been applied to the fabric, leave it to dry. Place the fabric on a baking tray in a low temperature oven for 10 minutes or iron outside or in a well-ventilated area until the devoré paste turns brown. Then gently hand wash in warm water until the burnt marks fall away.

Above *Coral Marks* (detail).

Below Burnt holes (details).

BURNING HOLES

Holes can be burnt into fabric or paper using a soldering iron. It is easier if fabric is stretched taut. Try to burn outdoors, but if working inside, do it in a well-ventilated room and wear a mask.

When working on very lightweight fabric or paper, incense sticks make lovely holes with slightly burnt, brown edges. Gently touch the burning incense stick to the surface – do not press hard or it will be extinguished. The papers can be joined to other surfaces using acrylic matt gel, while fabric can be stitched, pinned or bonded to other fabric, or incorporated with collage.

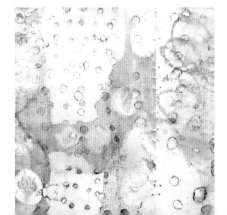
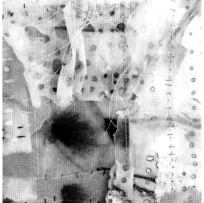
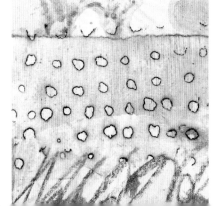

MAKING CHANGES

Cloth can be altered using methods such as weathering, abrasion, burning and distressing. To explore and replicate these processes, I worked on a series of samples made from a mix of natural and man-made fabric and thread, which were cut from one large piece of patched, layered cloth. Each sample has a slightly different composition but is made from the same fabric, thread and combination of hand and machine stitching.

Above and opposite The twelve samples before and after alterations. 28 x 14cm (11 x 5½in) each.

Altering twelve samples

Sample 1: Unchanged The original cloth without any alteration.

Sample 2: Repeated washing Washed 100 times in a washing machine.

Sample 3: Abrasion Abraded using wire brush, metal file, grater and sandpaper.

Sample 4: Burning Setting fire to the edges, then extinguishing; smoking damp fabric with a candle flame; making marks and holes using a soldering iron, incense sticks and a wood-burning tool.

Sample 5: Weathering Hung on the washing line for nine months.

Sample 6: Boiling and dyeing Boiled in a rusty wok, then wrapped with leaves dipped in iron water and re-boiled.

Sample 7: Staining Wrapped around a rusty object and tied with iron wire before wetting and leaving outside for two weeks.

Sample 8: Burying Left in a compost heap for six weeks.

Sample 9: Soaking Placed in a salt-water solution and left for eight weeks for the water to evaporate allowing crystals to form.

Sample 10: Cutting Slashing using a knife and seam ripper before repairing with stitch.

Sample 11: Making holes Using devoré paste to create holes.

Sample 12: Distressing Using an embellisher machine and felting needles to change the surface.

Samples numbered from left to right, top to bottom.

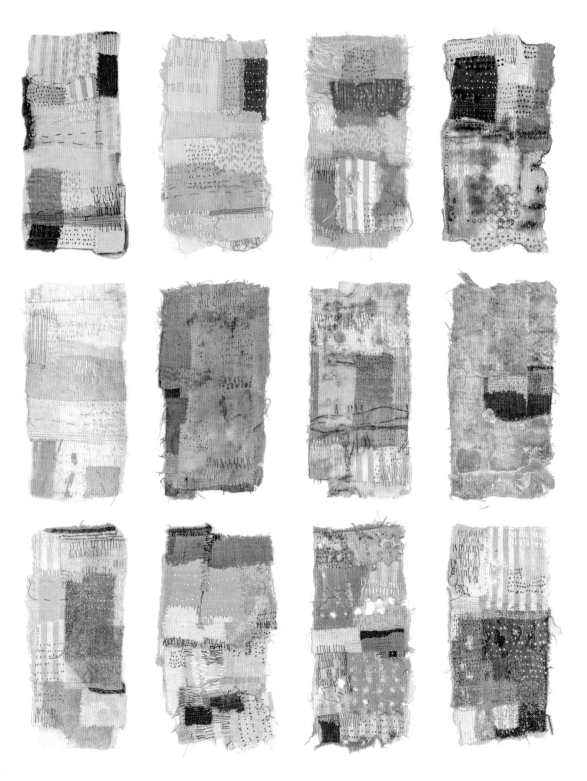

'I want to see scars, failure, disorder, distortion.'

Yohji Yamamoto

Some of these processes produced far more exciting results than the original. Of course, combinations of all of these methods can be applied to the same piece. For instance, holes could be made using devoré paste, then a wire brush used to distress the edges before being partially left in a salt-water solution. A piece of work can be altered many times, creating dynamic, innovative results.

FRAGMENTATION

How far can something be fragmented until it falls apart?
I like to distress fabric but it can be difficult to know when
to stop before going too far (see Burying, page 30).
Once a piece has become very fragile, it may need
repairing and strengthening to make it more durable
(see Repair, page 82).

FRAGILITY

Marked was made using lightweight and sheer fabrics. Parts were stained by
wrapping the cloth around rusty objects, while other pieces of the cloth were
screen printed. The fabric was fragmented, then patched and repaired. Rather
than cutting, I used an embellisher machine to divide the cloth. The repetitive
motion of the barbed needles distressed the fabric, breaking down the woven
fibres, making it fragile and easy to tear apart. It was easy to make holes in the
transparent, lightweight cotton organdie. The cloth was also reconstructed using
the embellisher machine, needle punching fragile scraps to the base fabric. Further
repairs were made using fine thread and hand stitching (see image on page 15).

'Only those who will
risk going too far can
possibly find out how
far it is possible to go.'

T. S. Eliot

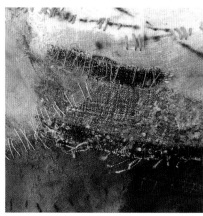
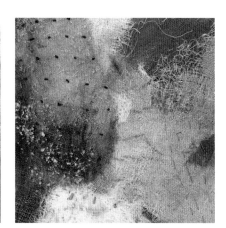

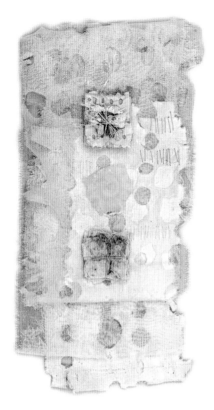

Small fragments of cloth and thread can be trapped between layers of water-soluble film, such as Aquabond, which is sticky and holds everything in place while working. The snippets are held in position within the film sandwich, then stitched together, and when the film is washed away, only the stitching remains, revealing a very fragile structure.

Coral Cloths is a series of work made in response to the devastating bleaching events of the world's coral reefs. Holes were made in the fabric using devoré paste and by hand cutting with small, sharp scissors (see Making Holes, page 36). Different weights of fabric were used, including very lightweight and sheer. The fragmented pieces were joined using hand stitch to create new large cloths. I made the work virtually colourless to represent the bleached coral. Washing added to the fragility, making the cloths very soft and translucent in parts (see Washing, page 28). They can be hung, gently folded, layered or rolled, yet still remain very light and fragile.

Opposite *Marked* (details).

Above Shelley Rhodes, folded *Coral Cloth* with fragments.

Above right Shelley Rhodes, *Coral Cloth*.
120 x 50cm (47¼ x 19¾in).

Jenny Bullen's recent work takes the form of fragile book structures. It has been inspired by walks along the shoreline – watching the birds on the mudbanks when the tide is out, observing the constantly shifting patterns made as sea meets land, and noting the ever-changing colours and marks left in the sand. She has a love and respect for kantha and running stitch lies at the heart of her pieces.

'Recently I have made a series of small, imperfect, concertina-type books, folding and creasing to make "pages". I like to use sheer fabric so that the stitches can be seen on both sides of the work as it is folded – the same stitch viewed differently. They are lightweight and delicate with a certain vulnerability. Although the work appears very fragile, I think textiles should be handled – so I display them on a plinth or shelf rather than as a wall hanging.'

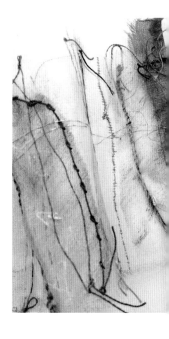

Above Jenny Bullen, *Fragile Book Form*.
7 x 130cm (2¾ x 51¼in)

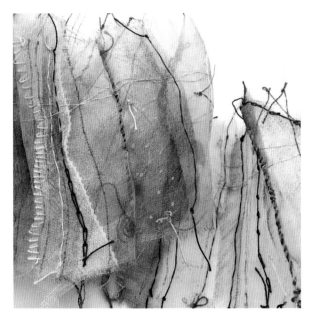
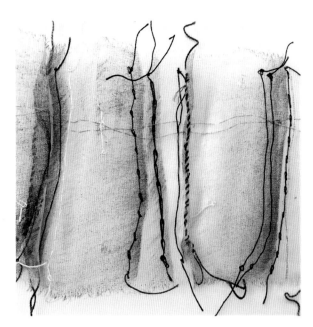

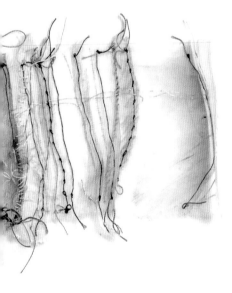

She works without planned sketches or drawings but aims to establish a sense of place in her work. She gathers fabrics together first – transparent and opaque, sometimes hand coloured and dyed, as well as scraps and snippets of commercially printed fabric. During this part of the process, she has a colour palette in her mind as she recalls a particular walk, as she explains:

'Although I like to draw and paint, I tend to stitch intuitively, working from instinct, recalling the sea or land, but do not have any drawings or images in front of me. I work without a plan, not really knowing how it will end up, but knowing that if I have put thought into the fabrics at the beginning, I should be okay. Sometimes I use one fabric for the piece, in which case I tend to apply fabric scraps as I stitch to add depth and colour. Other times I cut or tear fabrics and stitch them together as I work. I like frayed edges and often leave loose ends, which adds to the feeling of fragility.

For this series, I start with one long piece, then attach small scraps of coloured chiffon and indigo-dyed fabric. I try not to be too choosy as I select fragments, which I overlap and join with a few rows of running stitch. The repetitive, rhythmical motion of the stitching links to the movement of the sea. Occasionally, I punctuate the lines with a small cross stitch or French knot. I also love to over sew tucks or consciously pull the stitches to add texture to the piece. I use sewing cotton or fine silk thread so that the lines of stitching are not overpowering. When I consider I have the correct length, I may wax the piece if it seems rather fragile.'

Top Jenny Bullen *Fragile Book Form* (details).

WORK LARGE, THEN FRAGMENT

Many artists work on a large scale before isolating areas and cutting to make a series, or reconfiguring the fragmented pieces and re-joining to make a new piece of work. Fabric and paper can easily be fragmented by simply cutting, ripping or tearing. A seam ripper is a useful tool for fragmenting cloth. Fabric can also be slashed or shredded using a knife or rotary cutter. A viewfinder can help the selection process: the simplest way is to cut two L-shaped pieces of card, which can be overlapped and adjusted to make a square or rectangular frame. Alternatively, try a more random approach by turning work over and cutting from the back, using the element of chance to decide where the cuts will appear. Edges can be softened or made slightly ragged through manipulation, using a wire brush or embellisher machine.

Working in this way is a great way to make a series, as the colours and marks belong together since they were all made at the same time. It also introduces a different scale, allowing for large, bold gestural marks, which usually do not happen when working on small pieces. I often use this approach with sketchbook and collage work. When working in my daily sketchbook, for example, if I make a drawing that doesn't quite work, I simply cut it up to make a series of smaller pieces.

Sticky labels

A fun thing to try is to work on a sheet of sticky labels in the same way as any other piece of paper, by drawing, painting, printing and adding text. Once finished, simply peel the labels off and rearrange. There is an element of serendipity as the fragmentation is already predetermined. Of course, the labels can be torn or cut further, in a regular or irregular way. They can then be reassembled, with spaces in between or butted up together, and they can be bonded to fabric or interfacing prior to stitching.

I worked on two sheets of labels, inspired by my beachcombing collection. I used them to create three different pieces of work and still have lots of bits left over that will end up incorporated into my sketchbook.

Below Drawings on sheets of sticky labels with found fragments (before fragmentation).

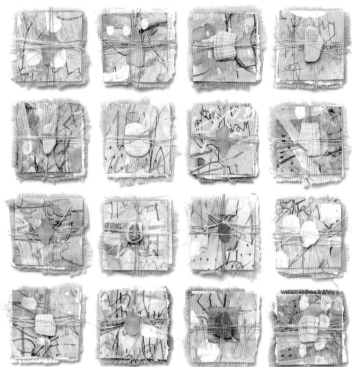

Above left Shelley Rhodes, *Bay Collage* (sticky labels). 30 x 30cm (12 x 12in).

Above right Shelley Rhodes, *Bay Fragments* (sticky labels). 30 x 30cm (12 x 12in).

Below Shelley Rhodes, *Bay Labels* (sticky labels). 23 x 35cm (9 x 13¾in).

Fragmented drawings

Here is something else to try. Make two
drawings of the same subject but use
different media or a slightly different colour
palette for each. Draw one by carefully
observing. Draw the other blind, without
looking at the paper; or use your non-
dominant hand; or work with a continuous
line. Cut or tear the two drawings, then
move the pieces around before re-joining
them, using glue, tape, stitch, staples, or a
combination of your choosing, to create a
disjointed image, before working back into
the fragmented drawing.

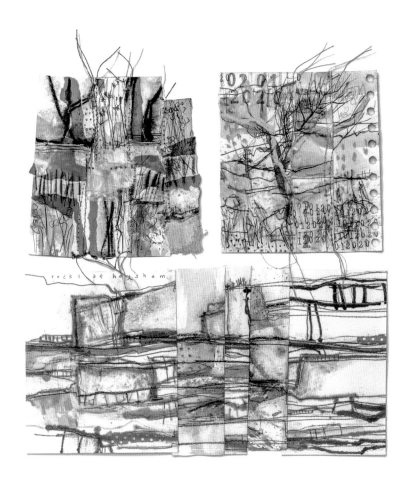

Right Sketchbook pages: fragmented drawings.

Opposite Shelley Rhodes, *Entangled Series*.
10 x 7cm (4 x 2¾in) each.

Garden Marks started as a black-and-white mixed-media drawing made on
a long strip of joined papers. I used a viewfinder to select areas before cutting
and tearing to create a series of smaller square pieces, to which scraps of
fabric collage and stitch were added.

Below Shelley Rhodes, *Garden Marks*.
Mixed-media drawings.
13 x 13cm (5 x 5in) each.

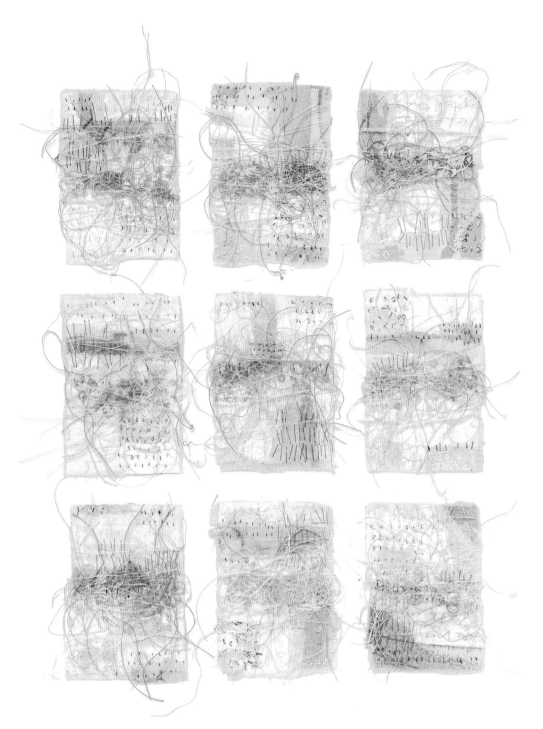

This approach of working large then fragmenting can be used when working with fabric too, as illustrated by my *Entangled Series*. I initially worked on one large piece of cloth, applying layers of acrylic paint, graphite pencil and ink onto calico. I worked quickly to create marks, allowing drips and splatters to occur. Sometimes I drew without looking at the surface and sometimes I used handmade drawing tools so there was some loss of control, helping to loosen things up. I often use text as a layer of mark-making but in this case most of the marks were text, although they were illegible. Choosing a neutral palette of grey and white to reflect the damaged reefs, I wrote about discarded plastic becoming entangled around delicate coral. Once finished, I selected areas and tore the calico to make 16 small pieces. I stitched marks, using my coral drawings as reference, and applied silver leaf to represent flecks of light and reflections on the water. This series looked okay, but I decided to fragment each piece further to represent the broken coral. I tore each one in two, then rotated, offset and re-joined each half to a different piece. I stitched the pieces together using plastic fishing line found discarded on beaches, leaving each piece entangled in a mass of discarded plastic.

FOLDING

Following a trip to Japan, I became intrigued by origami, the art of paper folding, which derives from the words *ori*, meaning 'to fold', and *kami*, meaning 'paper'. Folding changes which area of the surface can be seen, so working on large paper or fabric, then folding or pleating is another way to disrupt and fragment an image. I explored this idea by drawing and printing on large sheets of lightweight paper and sheer organdie before layering them, then creating tucks, creases and folds. I printed photographs onto copier paper and used them to add areas of collage. Once folded, some parts become hidden, and the position of one mark in relation to another alters. As layers are cut and peeled back, they reveal random marks by chance. Making holes allows glimpses of the layer below. Marks seen through translucent layers are softly diffused and slightly obscured. Areas may be waxed to add further transparency. Serendipity plays its part, but there is an element of control and choices still have to be made, as sections can easily be masked, hidden or revealed. Flaps and folds can be held in position using thread, pins, staples or tape.

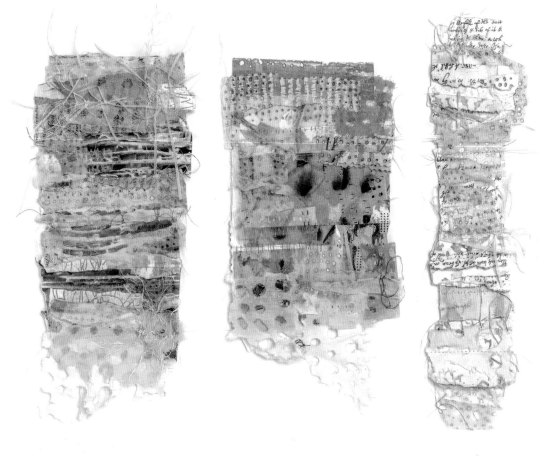

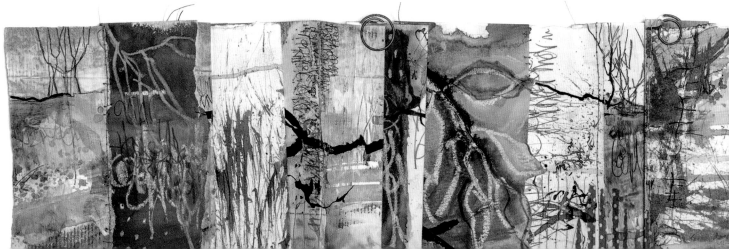

Folded book forms

Marks, drawings and prints can be made on large pieces of paper, which can then be folded into book forms. Chance happenings occur when the folds and cuts are made, as the image on one page unexpectedly ends up next to another.

Nine Folded Squares is one work from the series called *Reworking a Book* (see Dismantling and Reworking, page 72). Originally, I was making these collages into small origami boxes, but I really like the halfway stage of folding – particularly the unexpected juxtaposition of the marks. They can be continually flipped over, rotated or rearranged to change the whole look. They can be butted up together, or there can be gaps between each piece.

Occasionally, I take a folded strip of paper with me to record a walk. I do not always draw in a linear way, so the drawings, words and marks can jump across the folds. Sometimes, I rotate the paper to work upside down, or draw without looking at the paper. Some images overlap while other areas have spaces as I make the drawings without a predetermined outcome. These can be reworked when I get home by adding colour and further marks. They may be cut and rearranged by moving sections around. Sometimes I add collage and fragments gathered on the walk. The paper can be bonded onto fabric or interfacing, stitched and presented as a work of art in its own right, or it could be fragmented to use as collage, or be a starting point for new work.

Opposite, above Shelley Rhodes, *Ori-Kami* samples. Folded lightweight fabric and paper.

Opposite, below Shelley Rhodes, *Folded Walk Strip*. 14 x 94cm (5½ x 37in).

Above right Shelley Rhodes, *Nine Folded Squares (Reworking a Book)*. 38 x 38cm (15 x 15in).

Right Shelley Rhodes, *Folded Books*.

Folding, hiding, revealing and so disrupting and fragmenting the image lies at the heart of the work of Matthew Harris. His approach is principally one of excavation – almost archaeological in the way it facilitates the unearthing, sifting, sorting and ultimately reconfiguring of both physical and visual material. He describes it as 'a ritual of making that alternates between action and reaction, expansion and contraction, whereby imagery becomes compressed, buried, opened up and then revealed.'

His inspiration often comes from discarded or overlooked scraps or fragments. The starting point for *Cellophane Series* was a small scrap of folded and squashed cellophane that he found on the street. He peeled it open, made some drawings and notes, then refolded it and stitched it to a card to use for reference, as he explains:

'More often than not the work begins with a chance find. A small scrap of something – something ephemeral and everyday. Often discarded – usually found on the floor. These scraps are then undone, unfolded, picked apart and put back together again in an attempt to understand what they once were and how they have come to be what they now are. From these scraps, I make groups of drawings. From groups of drawings, I start to paint cloth, four layers of cloth, each painted with the same image. Then begins a process of folding and pleating, whereby these layers of duplicate visual information are sandwiched together to form strata of compressed and embedded imagery; a multi-layered cloth with heft, "seeded with potentiality".'

Once he has reached this stage, he is able to start excavating through the layers to reveal the fragmented image.

Top right Matthew Harris, *Blue Cellophane Cloth.*
43 x 49cm (17 x 19¼in).

Centre right Matthew Harris, *Cellophane Fragment.*
28 x 29cm (11 x 11½in).

Right Matthew Harris, *Bric-a-Brac Cloth No. 2.*
118 x 78cm (46½ x 30¾in).

Opposite Matthew Harris, *Bric-a-Brac Cloth No. 2* making sequence.

'As I cut through, shapes, lines, areas of colour and texture are exposed and a playful movement begins. Some elements I keep and leave where they are, others I move, sometimes slightly, other times from one side of the cloth to the other; some I expose and then bury again as they seem unnecessary. As this process plays out, I pay close attention to the material, responding quickly at times and more slowly at others, until eventually a composition begins to emerge. It has its roots deeply embedded in the original painted cloth but it has evolved to become a new image, reconfigured and pieced together. This process allows for infinite possibility and variation explored within the confines of the original material.'

He often makes work in a series of three or more pieces, all of which start from the same image. He likens it to jazz improvisation around a standard tune, where 'elements of the original remain but often they are only glimpsed or heard as fragments within the new.'

EMOTIONAL FRAGMENTS

Fragmented and repaired cloths can be used as a metaphor for grief and loss. Beverly Ayling-Smith uses this approach in her work, as she explains here:

'I use a poetic narrative and through repetitive hand stitch and slow processes, I aim to imbue cloth with emotion. My choice of materials is of great importance – most of my work uses torn fabrics, some as fragments and others patched and mended, reflecting on the small steps we take to overcome life events. I have used lead and linen in my work because of their association with burial. I am currently using Second World War army field hospital bedsheets as the main fabric for my work. They have special significance to me as one of my family members was injured and hospitalized in France shortly after D-Day.'

Wall of Memory is made from one of these sheets. It has been torn and mended, stained with bitumen to resemble a stone wall, and it is backed with letters written to her by close family and friends who have died. The tears in the fabric partially reveal the writing and are repaired by hand and machine stitch, to secure and hold them in place.

Beverly Ayling-Smith,
Wall of Memory
(details).

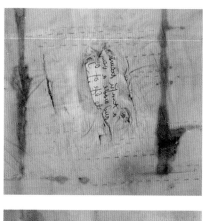
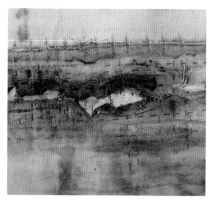
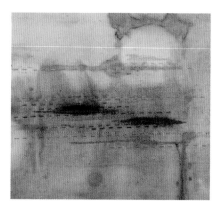
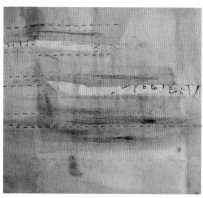
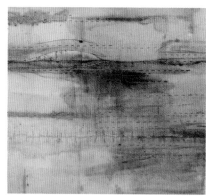
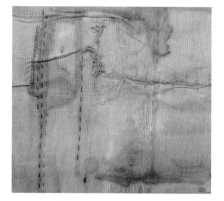
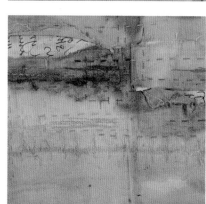
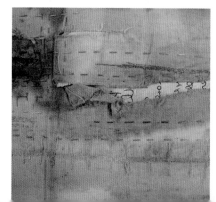
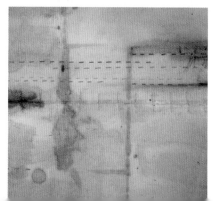

The Sorrow and the Pity is made from a type of linen that was used historically to make winding sheets, which were the original form of burial shroud: after death the winding sheet – usually a single bedsheet – was first laid on the stripped bed and the corpse placed on top; the sheet would then be folded around the body before being stitched or pinned in place.

'The linen in these pieces was torn and reconstructed using hand and machine stitch to create a diptych – one black and one white – which reflect on the extremes of emotion in grief – despair and resolution. The regular hand stitch acted as a form of meditation.'

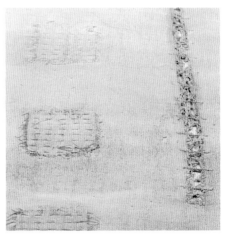

Memories, Dreams and Tears is made from two pillowcases which were torn, repaired, painted with bitumen and covered with ash. Nails were hammered into the surface and connected by a web of linen threads. Of this work, Beverly says:

'The work reflects on the intense emotions experienced when in contact with bed linens. Pillowcases bear witness to passions spent before sleep and dreams forgotten on waking. Although we endlessly strive to clean and launder them, they remain keepers of our memories, dreams and tears.'

Above Beverly Ayling-Smith,
The Sorrow and the Pity (details).

Below Beverly Ayling-Smith,
Memories, Dreams and Tears (details).

The London Foundling Hospital

This hospital was established in the mid-eighteenth century to admit and care for impoverished children whose mothers could not look after them. Mothers were encouraged to leave a token, such as a note or small object, so that if circumstances improved and they were able to return to collect the child, this would help with identification. Items given include keys, brooches, rings, watches and buttons, but the overwhelming majority of objects left were swatches of textiles – fragments of cloth, snippets from an apron, a dress or an underskirt. Perhaps a bit of ribbon, bonnet or sleeve cut from whatever the child was dressed in when they were left. Sometimes these were stitched with initials, birth dates or the place of birth. They were carefully pinned onto registration documents recording each child's admission to the hospital. A historical document but also an emotional token, each scrap is beautiful yet poignant, reflecting the life of a vulnerable child and a desperate mother.

If Only was made in response to these archival fragments. Made using snippets of baby clothes donated but never needed, it represents the sense of loss and longing by women who may have tried to conceive but never had a child of their own. It uses tiny baby pins and text in the form of letters written to unborn children. Each assemblage is wrapped, cocooned and cherished. Some are coated in wax, as a metaphor for protection. Pieces can be presented individually, laid out as a group or bundled together in a way that is reminiscent of a stack of carefully saved, precious hand-written letters.

Above Shelley Rhodes, *If Only.*
23 x 30cm (9 x 12in).

Opposite Cloth tokens from the London Foundling Hospital, which continues as the children's charity Coram.

FRAGMENTING TEXT

I often incorporate words and asemic writing within my work, treating it as another form of mark-making. Text can look exciting and intriguing when scrawled and illegible. These marks can be fragmented further and reconfigured. Rosalie Gascoigne created large-scale graphic images of disjointed text made from recycled road signs. They were cut, rearranged and assembled to create an imposing grid of fragmented letters and words.

Sharon Brown works with text and handwriting found on historic documents. She is drawn to the personal histories contained within them and intrigued by the shapes and rhythms of the letterforms, as well as the spaces created between each line of text. Recent work has been made using old letters and documents rescued from a cotton mill in Rochdale, which she found on a market stall. She felt a sense of responsibility to give these a new purpose, to show a way of life that no longer exists while revealing glimpses of personal stories relating to the characters as well as the history. She describes her process here:

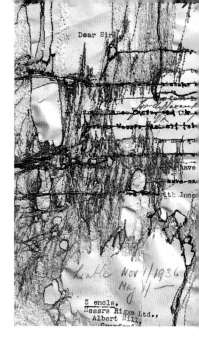

'The letter or document is pinned to a piece of calico and pulled taut in a hoop. As I begin stitching, the document itself seems to suggest how I should respond to it with my sewing machine. The physicality and speed of my movements mirror the direction, angles, style and energy of the text. Once the paper is secure enough, the pins get removed. This means that the paper doesn't always remain completely flat, becoming distorted, creating raised textural areas like contours or areas of relief. The freehand machine embroidery breaks down the fragile surface of the aged paper embedding it into the cloth with layers of thread. I try hard to hold onto the essence and authenticity of the original text but I also want new elements to emerge that are unplanned, so the work develops in a free and organic way. There is an ongoing tension between control, freedom and serendipity.

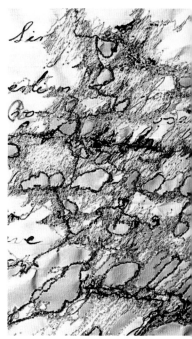

There are elements of destruction, distortion and fragmentation that I can't control as the needle breaks up the paper and text, forcing me to make new creative decisions about how and where I stitch. Some areas become worked to such an extent that any further stitching is impossible, or areas emerge that are so fragile that there is a balance to be struck between what to destroy, save or repair.

At some point the work starts to take on a life of its own. It becomes less about the original document and more about how I resolve it as a piece of art.'

Sharon Brown, *Riggs of Rochdale Series* (details).

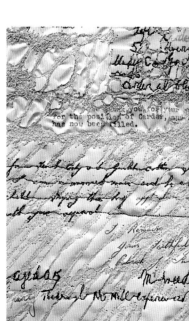

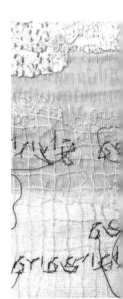

The Red List is a piece that I created to draw attention to threatened and endangered coral species, so named because there were 25 corals on the IUCN (International Union for Conservation of Nature) Red List of Threatened Species when I made the piece. I hand stitched the scientific names of the endangered coral in red thread on a predominantly white ground. The cloth was pieced and fragmented with repairs to represent the damaged coral and the fragments were held together with stitched marks relating to patterns, marks and textures found on the coral. While sampling and testing the stitched letterforms, I realized that I preferred the reverse side. It was still recognizable as text, but it became illegible, half-hidden with lost meaning. I thought this was poignant – a representation of the terrible loss of a species – so decided to hand stitch all the text from the reverse side.

Top Shelley Rhodes, *The Red List*.
150 x 18cm (59 x 7in).
Details shown above.

FRAGMENTING PHOTOGRAPHS

Photographs can be a great source of inspiration as well as reference for work, but they can also be fragmented, reassembled and worked on directly. David Hockney made large disjointed images in his series of photographic collages, in which multiple individual photographs were reassembled to make a new, slightly fragmented image. Michael Mapes takes this a stage further with his fragmented photographs that have been dissected and reassembled like scientific, entomological specimens. In his methodical work, he classifies and organizes hundreds of fragments to create three-dimensional collages.

Siân Martin uses photographs to create work with personal and emotional connections. The process of fragmentation followed by reconstruction enables her to transform rigid photographs into fragile, draping cloths. She tears and recycles old photographs then joins the individual pieces to create a new 'textile', linked by fine lines of machine stitching, which she describes as 'a sort of airy lace that moves and drapes gracefully'.

'I have explored many different ways of linking these small pieces – sometimes as a single layer, other times as three-dimensional stacks or bundles wrapped with wire or string. The little blocks can be stitched to a ground, but I prefer to make a free-hanging textile by threading them together, passing a continuous wire between the central layers of each bundle. Then I pass further lengths of wire through each piece in the opposite direction, connecting up the "warp" with the "weft".'

In *Family Ties* Siân uses torn fragments from a collection of duplicate family photographs, discovered when the family home was being dispersed.

Above Siân Martin,
Family Ties.
100 x 40 x 20cm
(39¼ x 15¾ x 8in).

Opposite, above Siân Martin,
Between Me and the Sky. 100
x 250cm (39¼ x 98½in).

Below Siân Martin,
fragmented photographs
(details).

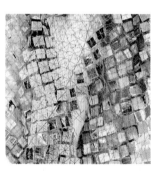

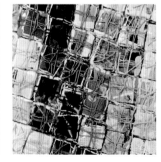

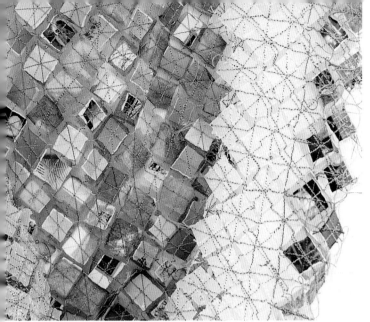

'As I tear the old photographs into stamp-sized fragments, I reminisce about the family occasions when each was taken. The torn shapes with their rough edges are organized into groups. I delight in sorting them according to colour, grading them tonally too if possible, giving me a wide palette of little piles to select from. The inclusion of vellum fragments denotes the paper my father used in his work as a technical engineering draughtsman. Each tiny fragment is cherished, lovingly reused and stitched together to make a continuous circular textile. Bands of colours represent individual parents and I have used the translucent section to unite the two colours and represent their joint life-long career in art and design.'

Siân joins the small fragments by machine stitching across one torn square at a time, then continues to stitch through thin air as the stitching travels from one small piece to the next, as she says:

'The mesmeric continuity of this stitching process makes it quite difficult to stop. I have all my little colour piles close by and only stop when necessary in the middle of a fragment. I make many miles of continuous stitched "strings" and cut them to the right length afterwards. Linking the strings to form a lacy textile construction is fiddly. I need a large table to support them, so I can work out the order I'd like to connect them. I use a series of boards to extend my working surface until it gets big enough to trail over my shoulder – giving me an increasingly long veil, which grows across my workroom floor.'

In *Between Me and the Sky*, Siân combines 'positives' from old slide transparencies with silk organza and linen thread. The translucent materials allow light to pass through the work, casting shadows and projecting tiny images from the positives. The work is linked to the concept of horizons that continually change.

'This work evokes the colours of a setting sun through multiple images from my creative life – all the transparencies are images of my own artwork and the local landscape. The idea developed from an interest in the rhythms in the Somerset landscape, where skies form vast areas and the land narrow bands. The transparencies are threaded together with dyed linen threads and connected with simple hand stitching. This is a continuum of my passion for making textiles from non-textile materials, such as fragments of old documents, photographs and old transparencies.'

I often use photographs to explore a subject in greater depth. If I am working from a collection, I will photograph the objects – particularly macro details. This helps me to focus and explore my collection in a fresh way. Then I fragment the photographs, moving sections and mixing images together, before joining and working on top of them. These disjointed photographs can be scratched, pierced and sanded. They can be drawn or painted on directly, and small scraps of paper or fabric can be collaged to the surface.

Things to try

1. Tear one photograph into several pieces before reassembling in a different order.
2. Cut or tear several photographs and join a combination of different images.
3. Explore different joining methods – glue, stitch, staple, tapes, brads or wire.
4. Construct in a different format to the original rectangle.
5. Alter the reconstructed photographs by scratching, piercing or sanding.
6. Make further changes by applying media such as ink, oil pastel, chalk and acrylic paint.
7. Add collage – use fragments of recycled paper and scraps of fabric.
8. Cut strips then weave together to almost pixellate the image.
9. Create holes and spaces by tearing, piercing, punching and cutting.
10. Manipulate by folding and creasing.
11. Make bundles and assemblages by layering and wrapping.

These manipulated photographs can become works of art in their own right, or they may inspire new work or a new direction. They can be rephotographed and transferred onto fabric using a transfer medium or digital printing methods.

Below Shelley Rhodes, manipulated photographs.

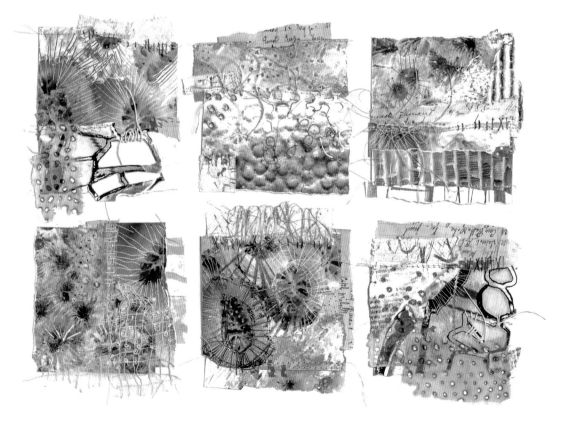

Transferring photographs

Once an image is photocopied or printed using a laser printer, it can be transferred to cloth using a specialist transfer medium. Basically, the transfer medium sticks the image to the cloth. I have tested many different products and several can be used for this process, such as acrylic medium and matt varnish; but for a fragmented, slightly imperfect image, try using household emulsion paint.

Step 1 Print the photo using a laser printer on regular photocopy paper (colours may smudge using inkjet copies but it is possible to achieve interesting results).

Step 2 Coat the surface of the photocopied image with paint, working quickly to avoid it drying.

Step 3 Place the paper face down on the fabric and press out any air bubbles so that the whole surface is in contact with the fabric.

Step 4 Leave to dry thoroughly, allowing the photocopy to stick to the fabric.

Step 5 Once dry, iron under baking parchment then spray the paper with water until it becomes damp. Then gently rub the surface of the paper away using your fingers.

Step 6 The reverse image is revealed – more often than not it is slightly broken and imperfect.

Above and below Shelley Rhodes, *The Journey Fragments*. These pieces use image transfer techniques.

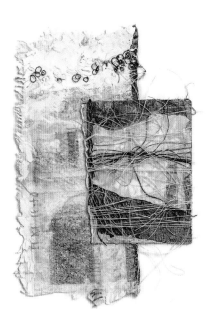

DIGITAL PRINTS

Photographs can be digitally printed onto fabric. Once the image is on the cloth, it can be altered, fragmented then reconstructed to create new work. There are specialist companies that will digitally print photographs on many different types of fabric, from lightweight organdie and chiffon to heavier weight cotton and calico. An image could be printed as a repeat pattern or increased in scale.

Alternatively, home printers can be used. Wen Redmond uses an Epson Stylus Photo inkjet printer with Durabright or Ultrachrome pigment inks, as she feels this combination produces the most permanent results on fabric (copiers use carbon, so are not permanent, and laser printers use heat so do not work well with the mixed-media substrates that she tends to work with). Her work is inspired by landscape and nature, using photographs taken with her phone. She often layers and manipulates several photographs prior to printing, using Adobe Photoshop, or similar software.

Wen takes a mixed-media approach, introducing a variety of media, papers, gels and paint into her printing process. Lightweight molding paste is sometimes lightly applied to interfacing, which adds texture to the printed surface yet still allows for stitching. Work usually incorporates recycled and reused papers and ephemera. These are fragmented and collaged, sometimes as a background over which a sheer piece of printed fabric can hang and other times to be printed on directly, as she explains:

> 'The base or substrate that I print on can include fabric, paper, interfacing or any combination of these – everything is considered. Any thin or floppy substrates need to be attached to a carrier sheet before printing, such as freezer paper. Silk organza is the only fabric I buy that is already digitally prepared for printing as it gives me light, transparent results.'

Prior to printing, the substrate is always coated with Inkaid – an inkjet digital preparation that helps to achieve clear and permanent results.

> 'In order to print large work, I divide the image into printable sections. Once printed and dried, I use fusible webbing to attach the prints to acrylic felt prior to stitching. Recently, I have been exploring more fragmented designs by cutting large quilted pieces into smaller sections, then re-joining using running stitch, overstitch or simply tying together. Edges are stitched or painted, which seals the threads, before the entire piece is coated with a protective varnish.'

She presents fractured images by overlaying and cutting, revealing glimpses of half-hidden pictures beneath sheer fabrics. Trimming and slicing allows fragments of the layer beneath to show through. Pieces of silk organza are printed and held using a few stitches so that they seem to float above the image below. Painted and handprinted fabric is sometimes digitally printed, and other times digital prints have paint and monoprints added afterwards. Further additions may include over-dyeing, printing or applying washes of diluted paint. The different combinations seem endless and there is always room for further experimentation.

Wen Redmond, digital print details.

DECONSTRUCTION/ RECONSTRUCTION

Items, including those made from fabric, can be dismantled by unpicking and dissecting before being put back together in a new arrangement, thus altering the overall composition. Deconstruction can be executed in a very careful, painstaking way, or things can be smashed or ripped apart more randomly. The separate pieces can be joined together with additions of other materials or by the careful selection of some parts while dismissing others.

'Every act of creation is first an act of destruction.'

Pablo Picasso

DISMANTLING AND REWORKING

Below and opposite Shelley Rhodes, *Fabric Book*. Made using recycled cloth. 13 x 17cm (5 x 6¾in).

Dismantling an object can be a great starting point for new work. This could be something that was discarded and found, whole or broken. It could be natural or man-made, old or new, hard, soft, mechanical or rusty. It could have an emotional connection: a family heirloom, child's shoe, garment, handbag or pocket watch. Once the object has been completely taken apart, the individual pieces can be used as inspiration for drawing and the dismantled parts incorporated into mixed-media work.

Fabric book

During the pandemic lockdown in spring 2020, like many, I spent time sorting and clearing clothes from wardrobes and drawers. As charity shops were closed, I decided to recycle and reuse the fabric. I took inspiration from Louise Bourgeois' fabric book, *Ode à l'Oubli*, in which she cut and fragmented her own clothes to make 32 fabric collages, reusing towels from her 1938 wedding to form the cover and pages for each collage.

I carefully unpicked and deconstructed sections of each garment before assembling some of the fragments into a cloth book. I took advantage of any areas that were particularly worn – fragmenting further before mending.

Small holes or threadbare areas were encouraged to grow, enabling areas of coloured cloth below the surface to show through. Pages combined different types of fabric in a range of weight, colour, pattern and texture. I made heavyweight double-sided pages interspersed with very lightweight single pages – a bit like protective glassine paper pages found in old books. Some fragments were pinned in, reminding me of old fabric sample books. There is something nostalgic about cloth books, perhaps invoking childhood memories of rag books. In this case, memories and narrative come from the recycled cloth.

Reworking a Book

Altering books is a contentious issue. Some people feel unable to tear up pages or destroy books. Having taken books to charity shops where they were politely refused, I prefer to reuse and give them a new life. The quality of paper and text in old books differs. Some paper is very thin and fragile, and some might be discoloured. They may contain delicate line drawings or illustrations, or have handwritten pencil notes scrawled in the margin: I embrace all of these things as I work on the pre-used paper.

The Library of Lost Books is a collection of altered books created by artists using books salvaged from stock discarded on the relocation of the Central Library of Birmingham (England). For this project, each artist was given a book to reconfigure. Some created sculptural pieces, others used the pages to make a new set of small hand-bound books, while some used the paper for printing or drawing on. It inspired me to create a new series of work from the pages of one book. I chose a book called *The Flower Garden*. The paper was fragile and slightly discoloured, with small text and lovely little diagrams and line drawings. I decided to relate my work to its content, using my garden as a source of inspiration.

I painted, printed and coloured some pages before folding them to create a set of envelopes reminiscent of seed packets, each one containing a small garden fragment (see top of page 131). I made a small concertina book, incorporating pressed leaves and flowers from my garden. Some of the papers were used to make a series of stitched collages. Leftover scraps were cut into small squares to make a mosaic-like collage.

Top Shelley Rhodes, *Concertina Garden Book*.
8 x 180cm (3¼ x 71in).

Above Shelley Rhodes, *Grid Collages (Reworking a Book)*.
20 x 20cm (8 x 8in) each.

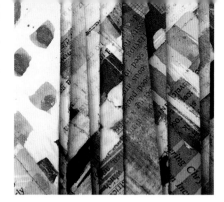

Above Shelley Rhodes, *Garden Boxes* making sequence.

Left Painted and printed recycled book pages.

Below and opposite Shelley Rhodes, *Garden Boxes (Reworking a Book).* 2 x 4 x 4cm (¾ x 1½ x 1½in) each.

I used some pages to make a series of origami boxes to hold a garden collection (see Folding, page 52). Objects gathered from the garden are presented in boxes, each made from a folded page. I arranged, bundled, wrapped and almost cocooned the items within the box, transforming them into protective nests. These can be displayed in a linear way, as a group or individually.

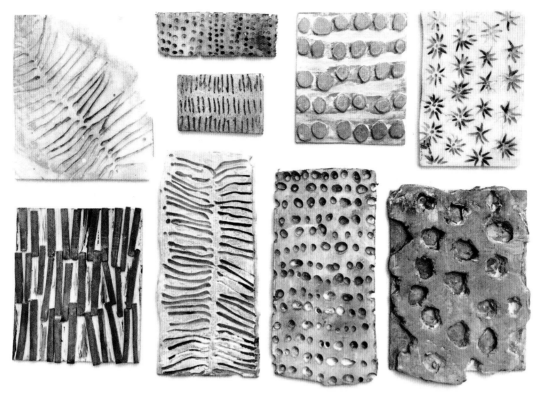

Things to try

Pages can be used in many different ways: a flat surface to draw, paint or print on; or folded, manipulated, woven, rolled or used in a sculptural way. Paper can be layered and stitched, torn and fragmented for collage, or bonded onto fabric. Once you have prepared a stack of papers, they can be used to create new work. Here are a few ideas to try.

1. Join pages to make large sheets of paper. These could be any shape or format. Recycled papers, scraps of old drawings or fragments of fabric can be incorporated.

2. Consider the joins, which can be glued, stitched or held with tapes.

3. Prime some areas using gesso or household emulsion paint – partially covering the text.

4. Use a wax crayon, candle or white oil pastel to make drawings, marks or rubbings that will act as a resist when further layers of media are applied.

5. Build up layers of colour using washes of watercolour, acrylic paint, ink, dye or stain.

6. Introduce text that relates to your subject – think of it as just another layer of marks. Write without looking, use your non-dominant hand, or try stretching or elongating each letter.

7. Turn your page as you work, so words and marks start to overlap.

8. Make your own drawing tools, related to your subject if you can (for my *Concertina Garden Book*, I found things from the garden). Use these with ink to draw on the large sheets of joined pages.

9. Stain, mark and dye the pages, using eco dyeing, natural dyeing and wrapping techniques, making bundles stuffed with leaves and bound with thread (see Staining, page 31). Try this on top of painted surfaces.

10. Make a set of simple printing blocks or stencils, or use a gel printing plate to create a series of printed marks (try reusing polystyrene packaging).

11. Alter some areas using media such as chalk, oil pastel, coloured pencils, charcoal or graphite.

Box Brownie camera

I dismantled an old Box Brownie camera and its case, carefully taking it apart and laying out all the separate components. Some were made into drawing tools, others were bound into bundles or mini assemblages, which I used as reference for drawing, mark-making and printing on a variety of papers and fabric (lightweight, heavyweight and pre-used). I also took photographs prior to deconstruction, which I incorporated as collage.

I made a series of small mixed-media collages, combining the deconstructed camera parts with the drawings and photographs. I introduced old slide mounts, which acted as frames, and vintage photographs relating to the old camera. Each mini composition can be presented individually but I chose to display them as a series of multiple units.

Shelley Rhodes, *Box Brownie Bundles.* 50 x 50cm (19¾ x 19¾in).

REWORKING WORK

Occasionally, I go back to finished work after a period of time to rework it; altering, deconstructing and reconfiguring to make something new. This could be making a series of smaller pieces out of one large piece, changing the overall size and shape by fragmenting, adding to or subtracting from the original. The work may have been for a specific exhibition or it could be too large to show at a new venue, or you may feel you want to change a piece because you have progressed and learnt new skills. The process of initially cutting the work can be difficult, but it is easier if you are unhappy with some part of it. Things can continually be adjusted and reworked but you will never have the original back, so be careful if you go down this path, and consider documenting and photographing each stage.

Regarding the new composition, I generally have a loose plan but I am always willing to deviate from it, remaining flexible and open to all possible outcomes. New fabric may be introduced: adding plain cloth will make an area seem quiet and calm, a flash of colour can draw attention, or an area of contrast may add depth. Not all alterations will be successful but they can be cut and changed again. Sometimes unintentional things happen that will surprise and delight – a fitting reward for being brave.

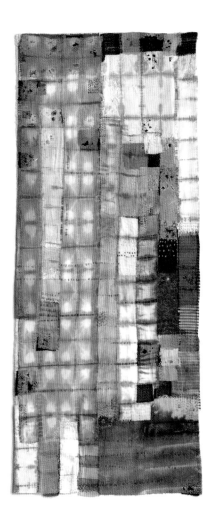

'Be brave. Take risks. Nothing can substitute experience.'

Paulo Coelho

Left Shelley Rhodes, *Reef Marks*
(before fragmentation).
146 x 59cm (57½ x 23¾in).

Above and opposite Shelley Rhodes,
Reef Marks Series.

Before reworking *Reef Marks*, I was apprehensive, so I started by cutting into my least favourite area – making two strips about 12cm (4¾in) wide. My aim was to create a series of smaller pieces, although at this early stage I was unsure of the exact dimensions. Decisions were made by continually moving and adjusting; some sections were fragmented further, then re-joined. The small compositions were pinned up, allowing me to stand back and assess the overall balance of the new pieces. Once satisfied, I pinned the pieces together before joining with hand stitch, although they could have been joined in other ways too, such as bonding, machine stitching, using an embellisher, or even a combination of methods.

New work does not have to remain flat – it could be manipulated to form folds, tucks or pleats. Two-dimensional work can be altered and reconstructed into three-dimensional forms to create vessels and containers. Consider not only adding to but also subtracting from the piece. Areas can be cut to leave a void; busy sections can be concealed with plain or sheer fabric.

Whilst reworking the new series, small fragments were left over. I saved all the precious scraps – nothing was thrown away (see Mottainai, page 138). These were assembled to create a series of smaller collages. Even the tiniest slivers were saved, which may find their way into a sketchbook, collage or a completely new project.

One small fragment could be the starting point for a new piece of work. Try placing a few fragmented scraps from a previous project in the centre of a piece of fabric, then work outwards by trapping little snippets beneath stitches and extending stitched marks. Work without a final outcome in mind and see what evolves.

Above Shelley Rhodes, *Reef Mark Fragments*. 50 x 50cm (19¾ x 19¾in).

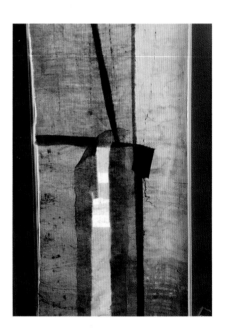

Jan Miller constructed *Light Veil* using different weights of linen and cotton offcuts, dyed together in a weak 'leaf stew with added walnut tree bark'. The cloth layers were wrapped and bound around a section of old bamboo cane fence, held together by rusted iron wire. The dried pieces were patched together using tailoring stitches, adapted from dressmaking techniques. The finished work was suspended in front of a glass door in strong sunlight. The already fragile colour faded even more and the rust stains and bamboo lines became vanishingly faint. So, Jan revisited the piece, as she explains:

'Two years later, I contemplate whether I should cut parts away to leave an abstract skeleton of the seams and apply to a new background … perhaps add "new" fabrics, paper or found vegetation to the faded cloth … or simply re-dye the whole piece, screen print or hand stitch. To explore new directions in textile work is exciting, but knowing that the original is lost, and that the replacement may be a disappointment, is inhibiting. I record details and thoughts in notes and diagrams, which seems to give it a history and me courage.'

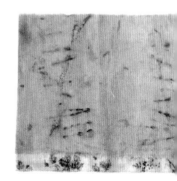

As Jan unpicked the seams, it fell in two. She worked on one half by re-wrapping the cloth around the same piece of fence, but this time using iron wire to bind the bundle, before boiling up in the original dyebath, refreshed with some florist's floor-sweepings. New stains from the iron wire that held the bundle together were fragmented, strong and inky black.

 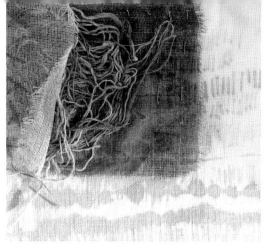 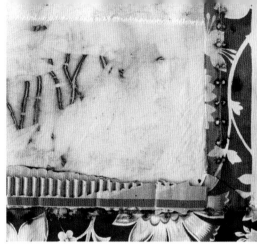

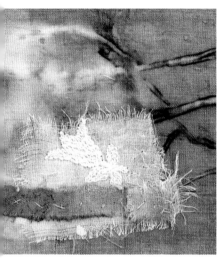 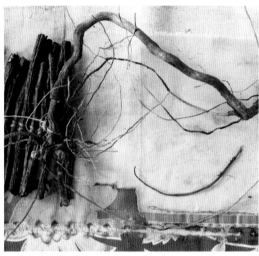 

Opposite Jan Miller, *Light Veil* (before reconstruction). 125 x 50cm (49¼ x 19¾in).

Below Jan Miller, *Light Veil Reworked.* 22 x 115cm (8½ x 45¼in). Details and notebook pages shown above.

'The broken fragility of these new marks reminded me of faded floral fabrics in my collection of early twentieth-century printed textiles. Old curtains and a bedroom screen – domestic pieces used to obscure both light and sight. I reveal the original vibrant colours as I unpick them to reuse. Which side do I prefer? Unpicked seams reveal original cloth and rings of rust around holes from removed upholstery tacks. Inside or outside; right side or wrong side? Original fabric selvedge binds, strengthens and defines the edges of Light Veil Reworked.

Presented flat on a table … floor … plinth and held down by a constructed "fencing" of twigs, roots and string – casting shadows that will gradually alter the surface of the reworked cloth. Working with my thoughts about light and fading; presence and absence; deconstruction and reconstruction; domestic functions of textile has turned Light Veil *into a new work – trying hard not to be mistaken for a contemporary table runner.'*

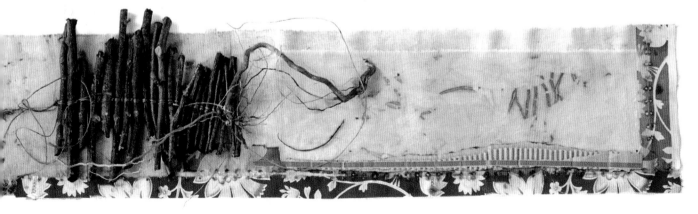

REPAIR

Definitions of repair include the terms 'to restore', 'to renew', 'to make good' or 'to strengthen'. I often stitch a repair, but also consider 'fixing and mending' in a more general way. For instance, I think about surgeons inserting metal plates and screws to fix broken bones. Could I use fragments of tin or metal to repair or join? Similarly, plaster casts hold bones in place as they heal. Home maintenance repairs may use nails, tacks, staples, glue, resin, bitumen, varnish or filler. Wooden splints can be used as a method of support before being bound or wrapped with string, twine, wire or tape. So, as I make repairs and reconstruct my work, I explore the use of these materials and techniques.

 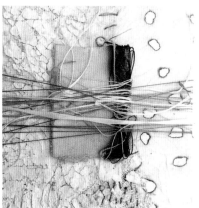 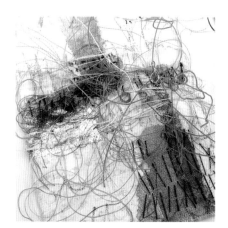

Above Details of repairs.

'I came from a family of repairers. The spider is a repairer. If you bash into the web of a spider, she doesn't get mad. She weaves and repairs it.'

Louise Bourgeois

JOINING FRAGMENTS

If something is delicate, fragmented or broken, there are ways to strengthen and reinforce it. Applying a layer of clear matt varnish gives stability and strength to delicate objects. Fragile fragments can be attached to a new ground in a variety of ways: they could be glued, stitched or pinned; they could be embedded in materials such as plaster, wax, clay or concrete; they can be wrapped, bound and joined using thread or wire; they can be trapped under sheer fabric, or held and contained within boxes, bags and envelopes.

Adhesive

There are many different types of glue: PVA, glue sticks, spray adhesive, fabric glue, starch paste, hot glue and superglue, to name a few. Acrylic medium, intended to be mixed into paint to alter consistency and drying times, also acts as a glue. I tend to use acrylic heavy matt gel medium. It acts like thick PVA glue but dries clear without any shiny residue. A liquid version called acrylic matt medium can be used to stick paper. However, the gel is particularly strong and enables me to adhere fragments such as shells, metal, sea glass and pebbles to surfaces, as well as sticking paper and scraps of fabric too.

Below Sketchbook pages with found objects stuck down using acrylic gel medium.

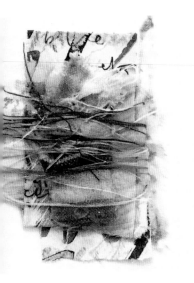
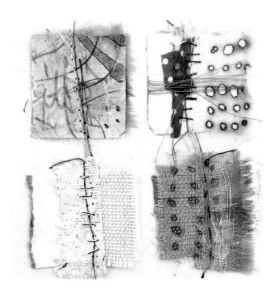

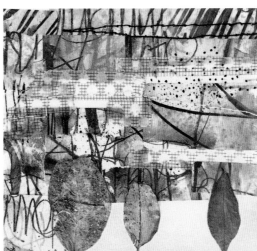

Pins

Fabric and paper can be joined and held in place using pins. Although they are often used as a temporary hold, I like to include them in my work as part of the finished piece. There are many different types and I seek them out in haberdashery and craft shops, as well as charity shops and hardware stores. I use them in a decorative way as well as a functional method of joining.

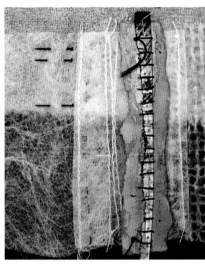

Left A selection of pins.

Above Details of work incorporating pins.

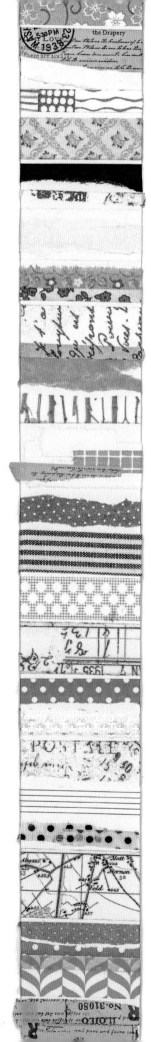

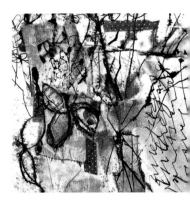

Tape

Adhesive tapes can be used to hold fragments in place. They are useful for joining papers but can also become an integral part of the finished artwork. Masking tape or microporous tape can be drawn, painted, stitched and printed on, leaving a slightly raised surface. There is a huge range of decorative washi tapes available, as well as brown gummed, linen and fabric tapes. It is possible to colour, print and draw your own designs onto tape by lightly tacking strips to plastic, working on the surface then gently peeling them off the plastic. All tapes can be torn or cut into smaller, irregularly shaped fragments, then used as another layer of marks within your work.

Fusible webbing

Fusible webbing is a man-made fibre that melts when heated. It can be sandwiched between two pieces of fabric then ironed, using a piece of protective parchment paper on top to protect the iron. The heat of the iron melts the fusible web and joins the two fabrics together. It can also be used to join paper to fabric; this will strengthen the paper and allow it to be stitched without tearing. Sometimes I tear off little pieces of the webbing and use them to hold fragments of cloth in place before stitching, instead of tacking or pinning. A reel of hemming tape can also be used to do this. Similarly, I often bond paper collage to iron-on interfacing to add strength and stability if it is going to be stitched.

Left A selection of tapes.

Above Details of work incorporating tapes.

Metal and wire

Scraps of lightweight metal can be used to patch holes or tears. Aluminium used to make drink cans is thin and can be stitched into, but great care needs to be taken as it is sharp once cut. Very fine metal mesh can be bought in craft shops that is almost like fabric. I like to find and reuse discarded, weathered fragments of metal. They can be glued in place first (using acrylic matt gel), then stitched across when dry.

Tacks and nails

I often use nails and tacks to hold fragments in place and they become part of the finished piece (as in my *Found* series: see Salvaged, page 22). Work needs to be attached to a hard surface in order to hammer the nails in. *Just as the Sun Shines Through* is a piece relating to the bleached coral on the Great Barrier Reef. The pins, small nails and tacks that hold the fragments of cloth in place also represent spawning coral.

Above right Shelley Rhodes, *Repaired Etching*.
Patched with metal. 20 x 15cm (8 x 6in).

Below Shelley Rhodes, *Just as the Sun Shines Through*.
60 x 20cm (23½ x 8in).

Plaster

Builder's plaster can be used to coat work, altering the surface. I mix it with household emulsion paint, PVA glue and water then brush it onto cloth (see Layering, page 132). These surfaces can be stitched before or after application. Plaster bandage roll can be used to bind and wrap – it could even be stitched first then wetted and moulded before it sets hard. Small fragments can be set in plaster if working three-dimensionally.

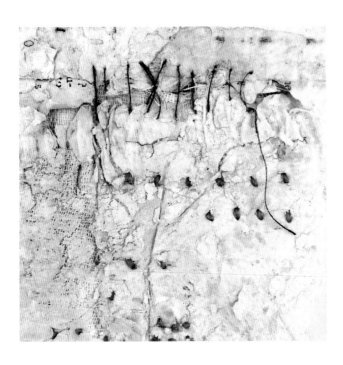

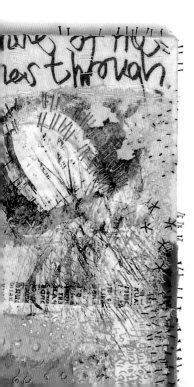

Above Cracked plaster sample.

Right Shelley Rhodes, *The Journey.*
Mixed media with image transfer and plaster.
85 x 36cm (33½ x 14¼in).

PATCHING AND DARNING

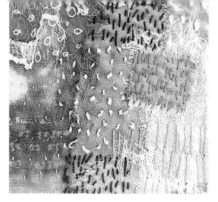

Patches of fabric have been used to repair garments and household items for centuries, usually out of necessity in order to make them last longer. Patching and darning can be invisible, or it can be used decoratively by employing contrasting colours, fabric and thread to highlight the repair. There is something poignant and beautiful about visible mends and repairs as they represent fragility, vulnerability and healing.

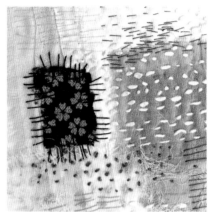

Conservation and historical ways of repairing and preserving cloth can be adapted to influence and inspire your own stitched work. Patches can be applied on top of a hole or placed behind it; they can have raw edges or be folded under; the fabric can be matching or contrasting. The patch can be lined up, offset, rotated or flipped. It could be lightweight on a heavy ground, or vice versa. Sheer cloth can be patched with transparent fabric, allowing stitches to be seen from both sides. Stitches can be decorative, dominating or discreet, worked just around the edge or right across the patch. Depending on whether you want the stitching to be visible or invisible, thread can match in colour or be contrasting – it can be thick, thin, shiny or matt. Explore and experiment – the variations are limitless.

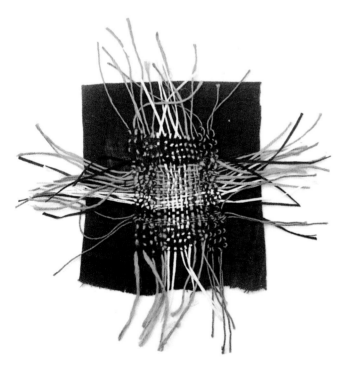

Threadbare areas can be darned. Hand darning uses a form of running stitch in which threads are anchored from one side to the other across the gap, before a second thread weaves in and out of them, criss-crossing over the hole until it is completely covered. Thread for the darning could be unravelled from the hem or the seam of the garment being repaired, making the darned area invisible. Using a similar but not identical thread will create a slightly textured surface, whereas using contrasting coloured threads adds a decorative element, highlighting and drawing attention to the repair. Threads can be left to hang loose, or stitched in and finished off neatly.

Above right Stitched repairs.

Above Darning sample with loose threads.

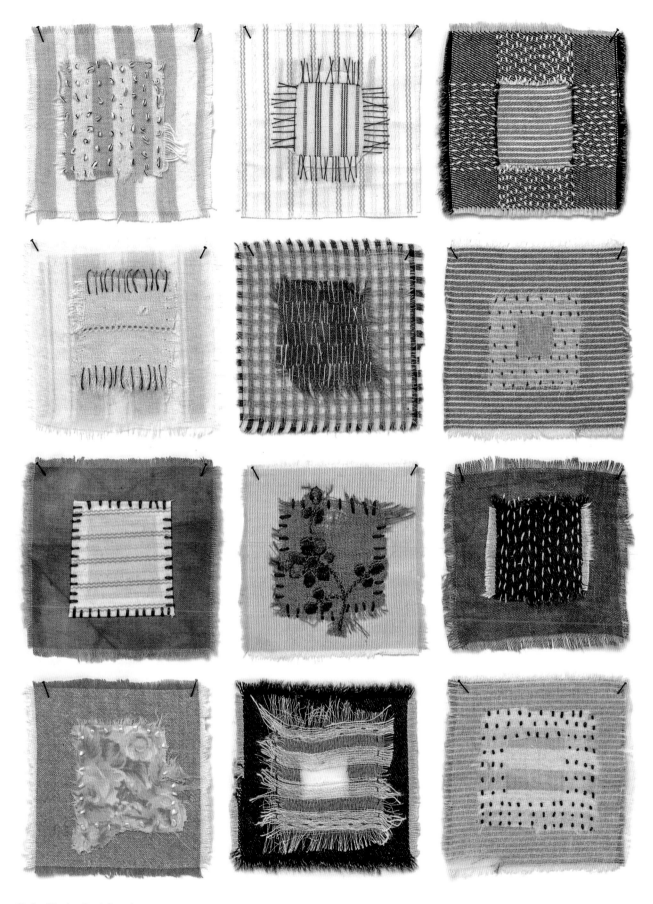

Shelley Rhodes, *Patch Samples*.
35 x 25cm (13¾ x 9¾in).

STITCHED MARKS

Stitches can join fragments together and repair holes but they can also be used to create marks. The colour and weight of thread, along with the direction and density of stitch, add colour, pattern, marks and texture to work. Small scraps of fabric can be trapped beneath the stitches. A huge variety of marks can be made by altering, distorting, exaggerating and extending the stitches. Consider the density of the stitch by stitching on top of stitches, as well as in both directions. You can change the look of the stitch by altering the tension, pulling tight or leaving everything loose and loopy. My samples show some very simple stitched marks using just straight stitch and two weights of black thread. Of course, all of these can be explored using a wide range of colours, different types of thread and fabric, and a more extensive range of stitches.

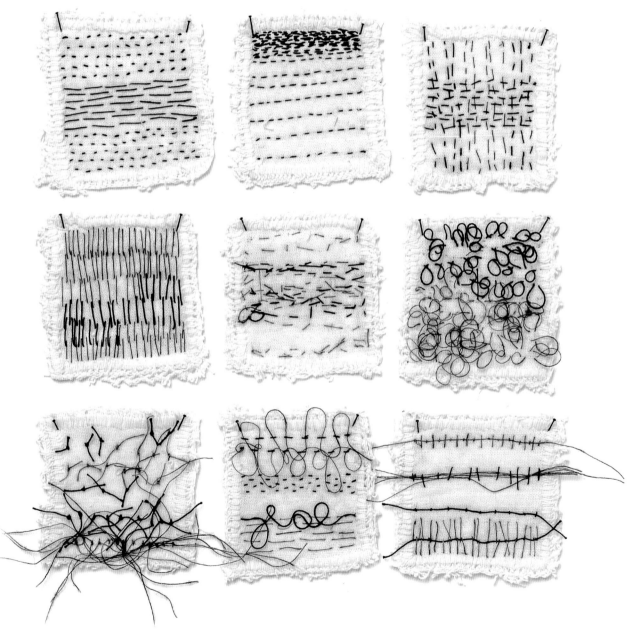

I usually relate my stitched marks to my drawings. When I draw and sketch, the marks are often full of movement and energy. However, when translated into stitch, they can lose fluidity and become rather stiff-looking. This is generally due to the length of time it takes to stitch. Although hand stitching can have rhythmical, meditative qualities, getting into this repetitive rhythm can make stitches look ordered and formal. So, I employ little tricks with the aim of making my stitches look more like my drawn marks, some of which are shown on the next page.

Stitch samples

Sample numbers go left to right, top to bottom.
1. Change the stitch length.
2. Change the density of stitch and the space between each row.
3. Overstitch in two directions.
4. Exaggerate or elongate a stitch.
5. Stitch without looking,
6. Change the tension, pulling tight or leaving loose and loopy.
7. Make single stitches and tie with a knot.
8. Loop threads around stitches.
9. Hold threads with straight stitches.

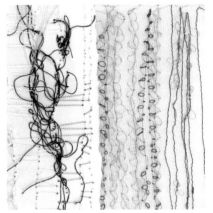

Opposite The stitched samples described above.

Right Stitched marks.

Below Shelley Rhodes, *Little By Little*.
Daily stitch practice (detail).

Shelley Rhodes, *Eco Strips Triptych*.
Eco-printed fabric fragments with blind stitching.
35 x 8cm (13¾ x 3¼in) each.

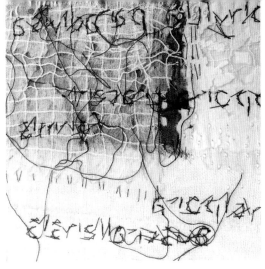
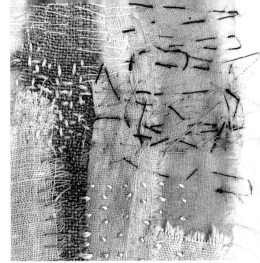

Things to try

1. Don't look at what you are stitching – this is quite difficult to do without peeking now and again, but I love the freedom of the marks.

2. Turn the work over and work from the back – this can create less regimented marks, as the 'wrong side' becomes the 'right side'.

3. Set a timer and work at speed – this often helps you to make less precise stitches.

Similarly, when I use a sewing machine, I generally try not to create perfect stitches or straight lines. I try to emulate my looser, hand-drawn lines and marks by altering the tension to make slightly loopy stitches. I stitch with speed, overstitch lines, stitch from the back and use free machine stitching, so that there is movement and energy to the stitching.

Above Stitch details: blind stitching, reverse stitching and speed stitching.

Below Machine-stitched samples.

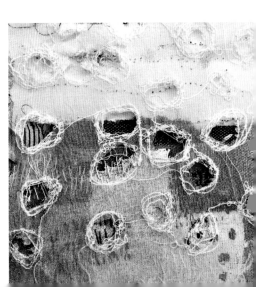

WORKING IN SERIES

I often work in series. I like to move from one piece to another as I make the work. I assemble and stitch in rotation, so when I feel unsure about what to do, I move on to the next piece. By the time I return to the original piece, I usually have some ideas about how to proceed. Every action leads to the next – simply adding one fragment of fabric or a few stitches alters everything. So, each piece is continually being assessed and evaluated, and decisions made accordingly.

MAKING A SERIES

Temple Market Series was made in response to the *boro* collection at the Amuse Museum in Tokyo. During my visit, I saw and handled an amazing collection of pieced, patched and repaired textiles – layer upon layer of tattered rags and fragments stitched together to make cloths and garments. Some areas were densely stitched, others had just a few stitches to hold a patch in place. I bought fabric in Kyoto's temple markets – indigo-dyed pieces and sections of patched garments, which I fragmented further before laying them out on postcard-sized pieces of fabric. Each fragment was carefully positioned by placing the scraps on each base in rotation. They were held in place by pinning and using tiny tabs of fusible webbing, before stitching the series in a rotational way.

Shelley Rhodes, *Temple Market Series.*
12 x 9cm (4¾ x 3½in) each.

The tiny leftover fragments were made into small, stitched compositions that I used to make a series of greetings cards (see Mottainai, page 138).

Left and above Shelley Rhodes, *Boro Card Fragments.*

Sally Payne often works simultaneously on multiple pieces which may lead to a series, as she summarizes here:

'Working on several pieces at the same time enables a collection to emerge that can share not only the original inspiration, but also take advantage of experimentation and accident.'

Sally's mixed-media figures are made from wire and clay, bound with scraps of fabric and thread, with the addition of found materials. The broken forms echo archaeological and other fragments seen in museums and elsewhere; held together with wire, they suggest shapes that may or may not have once existed:

'In this series, I have worked directly from the life model, reinventing relationships of form with abstraction. The decision to use wire and clay came after extensive testing of materials – air-dried clay and bamboo, varnished paper and fabric, scrim and plaster moulded into shapes. Beginning as quick studies in clay and wire, pieces were fired – some were broken and further breakages occurred during firing. This allowed for reconstruction, which included the use of gold leaf, thread, paint and paper. Wire creates new forms but also holds, binds and repairs. Figures are reimagined and reconstructed through the influence of archaeology and found artefacts. This series explores presence and absence, the unfinished, the incomplete.'

Below Sally Payne, *Mixed-media Figures*.
Approx. 40 x 18cm (15¾ x 7in) each.

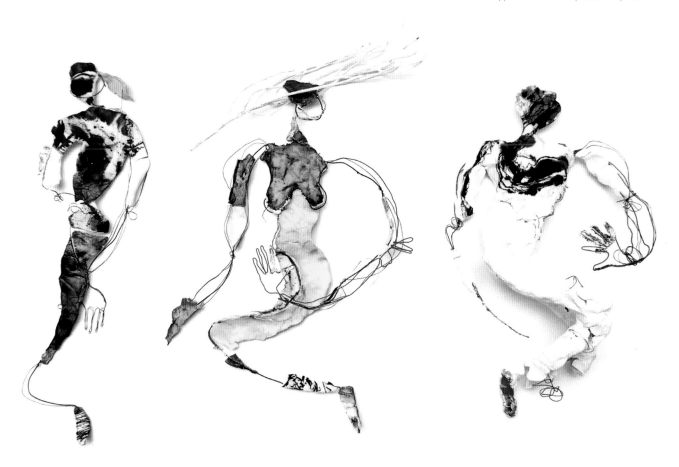

When working in a series, each piece can be a similar shape or size, but they do not have to be and they could simply be linked by content, material and colour. The series created by reworking *Reef Marks* consists of long thin shapes, squares and rectangles – they work as a series because they were part of one piece originally (see Reworking Work, page 78). Long thin strips attached to recycled buckles were created as a series, linked by their shape and colour.

Shelley Rhodes,
Recycled Series.
Fabric strips using
recycled fastenings.
45 x 5cm (17¾ x 2in)
each.

MULTIPLES

The use of multiples can be powerful and compelling. One small piece can look good – placing nine together may look more interesting, but increasing the number further can have even greater impact. Many artists have used this approach in their work, including Edmund de Waal with his large-scale installations of multiple porcelain vessels – white, ethereal, calm yet imposing. Similarly, Dutch artist Herman de Vries explored principles of repetition and the beauty of everyday objects in much of his work.

Right Shelley Rhodes,
Recycled Postage Stamps.
10 x 10cm (4 x 4in).

Above Wen Redmond, *A Day in the Woods.* 130 x 157.5cm (51¼ x 62in).

Wen Redmond's *A Day in the Woods* is made using multiple images of leaves. She used a combination of eco prints, natural dyeing, paper making and digital printing to create layered images. Threads tie individual units together to make one large work (see Digital Prints, page 68).

I take great pleasure in working in small multiple units. I naturally like to work on a small scale, so working this way always seems manageable and achievable. Small pieces are transportable and can easily be worked on anywhere using limited free time.

In 1967, French artist Robert Coutelas began working on his *Cartes* series. He used discarded cardboard and wood to create a series of tarot card-sized paintings with rounded corners, eventually making 6,000 small painted works depicting mystical, symbolic and medieval images. Inspired by Coutelas' work, Japanese textile artist Junko Oki made her wonderful series of small stitched pieces called *Culte à la Carte*. In response to Coutelas' multiple little paintings, I made my own series of mini cards with rounded corners. I used eco prints made on long strips of fabric and paper, exploring different outcomes using various fabric, paper and foliage. I altered the types of additives and mordants as well as the cooking times and dye baths. I was experimenting and testing new techniques, so while there were some beautifully printed areas, some parts did not print well, making it an easy decision to fragment and rework them. I made a template denoting the size of each piece, then selected areas from my large prints by cutting, tearing and fragmenting. Scraps of naturally dyed fabric were also included. The paper pieces were particularly fragile, so each collage was attached to interfacing, making it strong enough to stitch. In homage to Robert Coutelas, I called the series *Eco Cartes*.

It can be effective to make collages, mixed media or stitched pieces on the same small ground by recycling things such as old train tickets, playing cards, index cards, stamps, postcards, beer mats or photographs (see stamps on page 99 and *Specimen Cards* in Layering, page 132). From the 1960s, Lenore Tawney made postcard collages, incorporating illustrations from books and magazines, text, stamps and drawings. They were a regular postcard size and she posted them to friends.

Below Shelley Rhodes,
Recycled Train Tickets.
8.5 x 5.5cm (3¼ x 2¼in) each.

Shelley Rhodes, *Eco Cartes*. 8.5 x 6cm (3¼ x 2½in) each.

Only Five Percent consists of 100 small units, which I created as one piece of work. It explores coral bleaching resulting from rising sea temperatures, where algae on the surface of the living coral is expelled, causing the loss of its vibrant colours; the white of the limestone shell shines through the transparent skeletal bodies, leaving it exposed and much more likely to die. During my research, I was shocked to discover that 50 percent of the world's coral is already damaged, that 10 percent is damaged beyond repair and that only 5 percent is unaffected and in pristine condition. I wanted to represent these statistics in some way, so I made 100 individual pieces, each representing one percent of the world's coral. Half were made in shades of white and grey to represent the bleached coral. Colour was introduced to reflect the undamaged reefs, with just five of the pieces brightly coloured, indicating no damage.

The pieces included drawings and prints inspired by marks and patterns observed on coral – dots, dashes, circles and lines. Statistics, information and text relating to the damage were incorporated and printed using thermofax screens, block printing and image transfer. I distressed fabric and made holes using a variety of techniques (see Making Holes, page 36). The small fragmented pieces were joined together with stitch. The stitched marks echo the patterns on the coral. The work was shown in a touring exhibition. As pieces sold, they were replaced with a same-size replica image printed onto tracing paper, and these ghost-like images represent the loss of coral species.

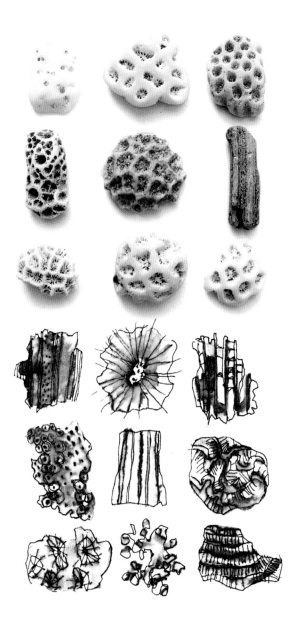

Left and Below Coral fragments and drawings.

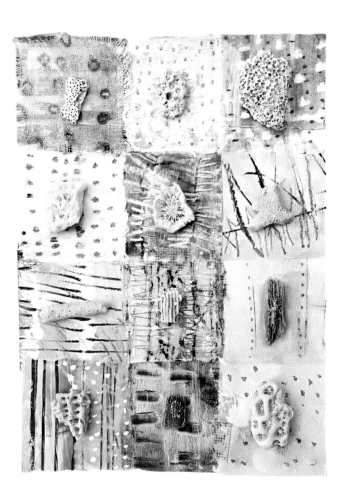

Shelley Rhodes, *Only Five Percent*. Detail showing 12 units from 100, approx. 23 x 13cm (9 x 5in) each.

PRESENTING A SERIES

It is possible to take a flexible approach with regards to displaying multiple units of work and they do not always have to be displayed in the same format. Alice Fox did this successfully with her exhibition *Findings*, in which she responded to objects collected from various locations (see *Tide Line*, page 34 and *Lime Kiln Objects*, pages 35 and 116), as she explains:

'Whilst many of my small pieces can be isolated and shown as individuals, they have particular impact in collections. Much of my work is shown in this way and I enjoy the flexibility of arranging the individual units differently each time or in response to the space and location. My exhibition 'Findings', of which the Lime Kiln Objects *were a part, included a few hundred small items, initially shown in a white-walled gallery space, presented in an archival way, as if they were part of a natural history or archaeological collection. The following year I showed the same work, but this time hung in a single line round a different gallery space. A further exhibition saw some of the objects grouped in grids, mixed up in terms of their provenance and material, and thus revealing new relationships between them.'*

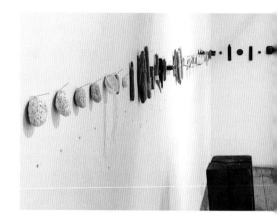

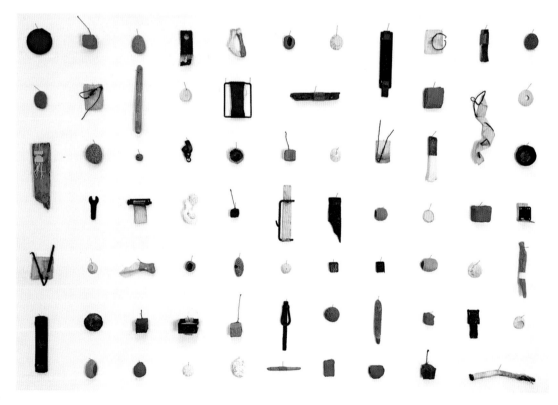

Above Alice Fox, *Findings*, displayed in different gallery spaces.

Beverly Ayling-Smith's *Mendings II* demonstrates the strong visual impact of multiples. The work consists of 333 small pieces of torn cloth, each damaged in some way and then repaired, either by darning, patching or piecing. Each small mend acts as a metaphor for the mending and healing process during mourning, making a person whole again. Seven different types of mending were used to repair damage to the fragments of cloth:

Above Beverly Ayling-Smith, *Mendings II* (detail).

1. Patching from the front with stitches over the patch edge.
2. Patching from the front with edges turned under.
3. Patching from the front with stitches contained within the patch.
4. Patching from the back.
5. Stitching torn edges together with straight stitches.
6. Stitching torn edges together using cross stitches.
7. Darning into the surface.

Beverly explains the significance of this:

'I often use the number seven in my work because seven people that I knew died in a short space of time, resulting in a difficult time for me. Using the number seven in my work is a way for me to hold them close and honour their memory.'

COLLAGE

The word collage is derived from the French word *coller,* meaning 'to glue' or 'to stick together'. It describes the technique as well as the finished piece of work, which involves arranging fragments of paper, photographs, fabric and other ephemera, then sticking them to a supporting surface.

A bit of history

The origins of collage go back to China and the invention of paper. From around the tenth century, Japanese calligraphers glued fragments of paper to a ground on which to practise their calligraphy. In England in the eighteenth century, Mary Delany created exquisite, detailed collages illustrating botanical specimens. During the nineteenth century, paper ephemera was used to make scrapbooks and homemade Valentine's cards.

Collage became very popular at the beginning of the twentieth century through the work of Georges Braque and Pablo Picasso, and later that century many artists, including

Kurt Schwitters, explored the medium of collage: recycling and reusing discarded paper and materials, which included bus tickets, fragments of newspaper, magazine clippings, broken items and bits of wire.

In the twenty-first century, American artist Mark Bradford has taken this art form to a new level with his urban collages on a monumental scale. He describes himself as an artist who paints with paper. Using found materials, he glues down layer upon layer of paper, sometimes embedded with rope, before tearing, peeling, gouging and scraping to reveal the multitude of layers beneath the surface.

  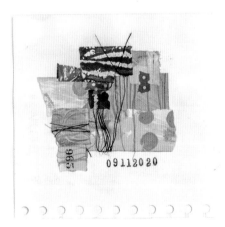

Sketchbook pages with collage.

FRAGMENTS FOR COLLAGE

The key to making a collage is the selection, positioning and modification of individual elements to create a pleasing and balanced piece. Then consideration needs to be given to how everything is held in place. Picasso often used pins to hold fragments of his collage in place. I also like to use pins, but stitch, tape or staples could also be used (see Repair, page 82). Collage can be attached to different grounds, such as paper, card, wood, canvas boards, MDF, Perspex or fabric. If I intend to add stitch to paper collage, I often attach it to interfacing, as it prevents the paper from tearing (see Fusible Webbing, page 85).

I think of collage as an extension of collecting – gathering all kinds of papers, ephemera, scraps of fabric and small objects for inclusion. I like to work with reclaimed papers, such as packaging and ledger pages, and generally I use what I have or what I can find. However, I do buy specialist lightweight papers, such as lens tissue and abaca paper, as these are difficult to source from recycled materials; virtually translucent, I can layer them, yet still see the marks beneath the top surface.

I usually colour and mark paper myself to use in collage; using my own drawings and prints is satisfying and personalizes my pieces. I also keep all the leftover bits from finished projects, rejected drawings, prints and sketches, test pieces and samples, as these can be fragmented and incorporated into collage.

Hannelore Baron's mixed-media collages incorporate torn paper, scraps of fabric, thread, ink, etchings and monoprints. Imagery includes stylized birds and figures, patterns and marks linked to hieroglyphics, illuminated scripts, musical scores and Persian miniatures. They are small and sensitive and have a quiet vulnerability that invites the viewer to look closer.

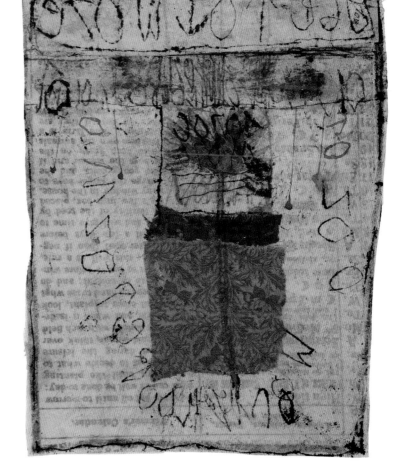

Hannelore Baron (1926–1987), *Untitled (C83285)*, 1983, mixed-media collage with fabric, paper and ink. 23.75 x 19.25cm (9³/₈ x 7⁵/₈ in), signed; © Estate of Hannelore Baron; Courtesy of Michael Rosenfeld Gallery LLC, New York, NY.

Wabi-sabi collage

Donna Watson is a contemporary collage artist who has been exploring her Japanese heritage for many years. While in Japan, she visits the temple flea markets, seeking out old books, letters, postcards, scrolls and kimono remnants. Her work, which includes collage, paintings, assemblage and book art, revolves around the Japanese aesthetic of *wabi-sabi* (see Discarded and Abandoned, page 16).

'I am drawn to the beauty of things weathered, worn, textured, rusty … objects and nature affected by the passage of time. My collages are nature-based, influenced by the seasons, cycles of life and renewal. I live on a cliff on an island, with wooded trails down to the beach below my home. As I walk, I constantly

forage for bits … I never come home empty-handed. My studio is filled with lots of different collections, from shells and stones, to seed pods, sticks and driftwood, nests, feathers, animal bones and skulls. I have bins and drawers full of Japanese washi papers, fabric remnants and strings. My studio is cluttered with my treasures, which I often incorporate into my collages, paintings and assemblages.'

She paints Japanese washi papers with acrylic paint, using a subdued, limited palette of mainly black, white and raw umber, with a few colours mixed in. The careful placement of each element is important as she looks to achieve balance within each piece.

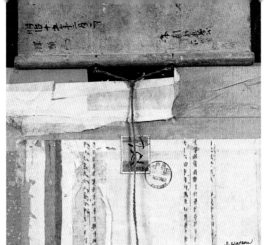

'I try to contrast light and dark colours, and textured papers next to smooth papers. My focal point is usually a nature-based image or found object. I create marks using dots, circles and crosses, as well as text and numbers. These marks are usually added at the end … placed where I think some interest is needed. Occasionally I use rubber stamps for this, or I hand paint them.'

Above Donna Watson, *Old Remnants Series*. 26 x 26cm (10 x 10in) each.

Her photographs for collage are made into solar etching plates, which ensures every image is slightly different due to variations of the ink, paper and press. She uses water-based printing ink on Japanese washi papers, such as mulberry, kozo and hosho. These are different from those she applies acrylic paint to, when she looks for more textured papers, like kinwashi, unryu or lightweight tengucho.

'I used to print my images for my collage on my computer printer but changed to solar plate printing two years ago because the computer-printed images seemed too mechanical and perfect; I wanted a more organic look – more in tune with wabi-sabi.'

Donna uses matt medium to adhere all the elements of the collage, before it is sealed with a clear acrylic spray for protection. She always works in series within the general theme of *The Passage of Time and What Remains*. The number of pieces in each series varies and may be as high as 40. Each piece within the series is connected by types of paper, colour palette, choice of images, content and text.

'When I work in a series, I make some decisions ahead of time – there is always some planning… but I cannot predict the outcome. Working this way gives me greater flexibility and by the time I have finished one series there are usually sparks of ideas for the next.'

Opposite Donna Watson, *Cycles Series*.
20 x 20cm (8 x 8in) each

Matthew Harris creates collages in the form of paper cartoons, which he uses to inform his work in cloth (see page 54). He paints, marks and then folds Japanese paper that has been waxed to make it semi-transparent. Once folded, he ties it to a backing board by wrapping a grid of thread, which is stitched into place, before working back on top of the image with oil bars.

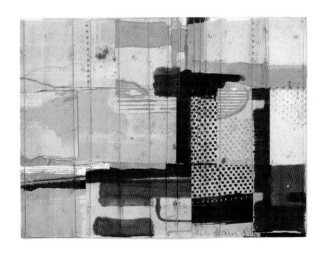

Right Matthew Harris, *Cellophane Scrap* (cartoon for cloth).
42 x 53cm (16½ x 20¾in).

DRAWING FOR COLLAGE

On a trip to Greece, rather than working in a sketchbook, I worked on separate pieces of A4 paper. I covered each sheet with drawings, marks and text. Drawing tools were made using things found on the beach, allowing me to scribble and splatter, building up layers using wax crayons, paint, ink and coloured pencils. I was not trying to create a finished piece of art as I intended to tear each page to use for collage. When I returned home, I isolated areas using a viewfinder before fragmenting, moving and joining different pieces together, using acrylic matt gel, washi tape and stitch to create a series of collages. I kept all the scraps and tiny leftover pieces and used these to make a set of tags and a series of small fragments on which I presented some of my beachcombing collection.

Right Greece sketches with drawing tools.

Below Shelley Rhodes, *Greece Beach Labels*.
25 x 42cm (9¾ x 16½in).

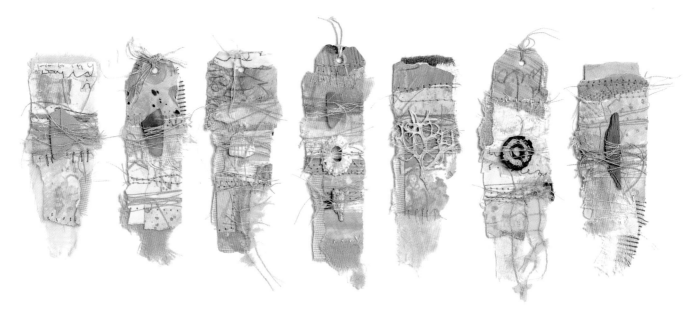

Opposite, above Shelley Rhodes, *Greece Beach Fragments*. 30 x 30cm (12 x 12in).

Opposite, below Shelley Rhodes, *Greece Collage Series*. 21 x 15cm (8¼ x 6in) each.

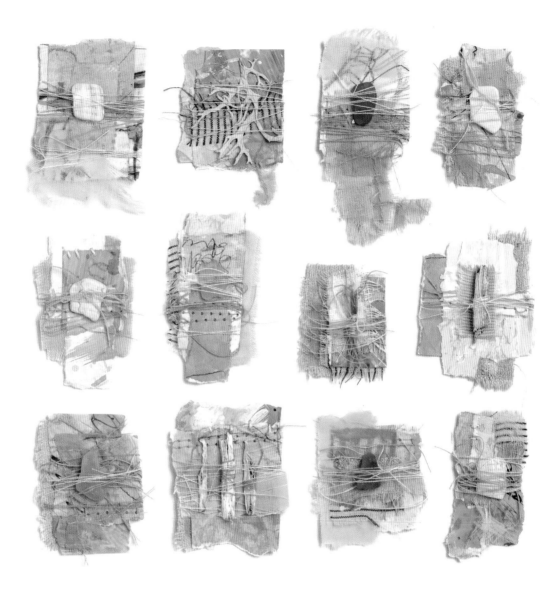

Turn a mistake into an opportunity

reed beds

I draw or print every day. It enables me to learn and discover – to explore innovative methods, to test materials or to try a new colour palette. Taking a chance can lead to new discoveries, but sometimes things don't work. I see 'mistakes' as an opportunity – a chance to alter and rework. I never discard a page completely but use it to push things further, turning it into something positive. By reworking these pieces, I have nothing to lose – so I cut, flip, move, re-paint or cover parts. Sometimes I join sections to make a new whole, other times I make mini compositions or thumbnails, which I may present in a grid format or make into little labels.

land marks

Areas can be hidden or cut out completely – subtracting from work is as important as adding to it. Simplifying, paring down, making an area calmer or quieter can alter a piece dramatically. Sometimes stains and marks that have seeped through to the back of a page are more satisfying than the front. Even when painted over, the history of your marks, drawings, colour – everything you have previously done – will still be there and hints of it may show though. These marks become part of the series of layers. Remember, you have the ability to alter anything you do, so be brave, take a chance, try new things, explore, experiment and play – everything can be altered, adjusted or changed. If a sketch looks very heavy, simply cutting it into a series of smaller pieces, rearranged with spaces between, can suddenly make it seem far more dynamic and exciting.

little labels

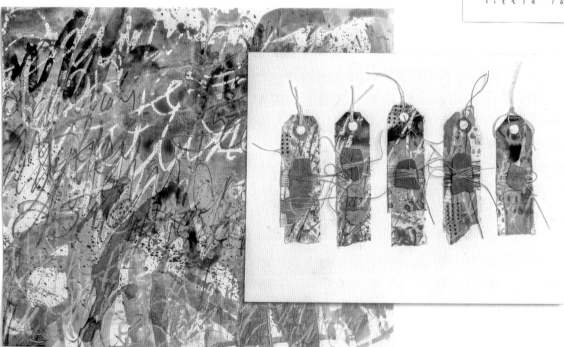

'Mistakes are the portals of discovery.'

James Joyce

Above Reworked sketchbook pages.

Left Fragmenting a sketch for collage.

COMBINING FABRIC AND PAPER

Cuban Windows was made in response to window shutters that I saw in Havana. I made a set of small paper collages to represent the shutter slats, which were attached to a base fabric to create a collage combining fabric and paper. The paper pieces were wrapped, pinned and stitched to the fabric ground.

Paper can be manipulated and used in a similar way to fabric. It can be torn, folded, pleated and layered. Holes or windows can be cut to reveal other layers. It can be bonded to fabric, stitched and joined in many ways. Paper can be softened by scrunching and crumpling, or it can be left outside to weather (see Weathering, page 25 and Manipulation, page 24).

Right Shelley Rhodes, *Cuban Windows* (detail).

Below Shelley Rhodes, *Times Nine*. 11 x 11cm (4¼ x 4¼in).

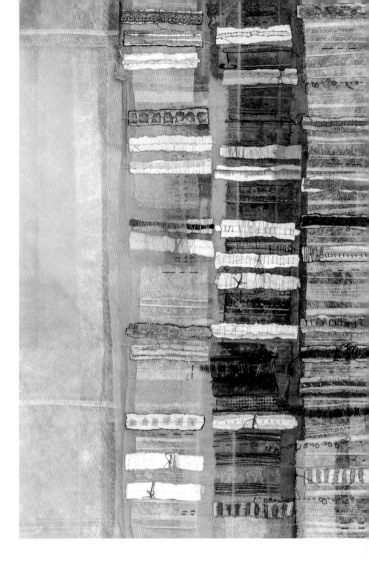

Times Nine is a series of collages made on reclaimed fabric and paper using a limited colour palette. I made a stack of decorated paper and fabric, giving me plenty of choice when putting each composition together. I isolated and selected areas before constructing them in an ordered grid-like format, although they could easily have been made in a more irregular way. When making a collage, there is an ongoing process of selection and modification, by moving and repositioning pieces. Introducing one new fragment affects the rest of the composition, so I stayed flexible, not committing to the final composition until everything was in position; then all the fragments were stuck down before stitching.

COLLECTING
FRAGMENTS

Many artists are collectors, accumulating materials and
gathering discarded, found and inherited objects – fragments,
remnants and scraps. I am no exception. Wherever I walk,
whether in the countryside, on the coast or an urban
environment, I am constantly picking things up. I am
particularly drawn to overlooked, broken and mundane objects.

I often return home with little treasures to be sorted, organized and displayed; curating my 'collections'
in boxes, on shelves or in reclaimed printer drawers. I use them as a starting point for drawing and
mark-making, as well as for extracting colour, pattern and form. Sometimes found fragments are
included in finished work. Occasionally the arrangement and presentation of found objects becomes
the piece of work (see Lockdown Walks, page 117).

Above Arranging
collections.

FOUND FRAGMENTS

I often use a collection to inspire and extract a colour palette for new work. Generally, I like to start with a limited colour palette (that does not mean it has to be neutral); additional colours can be introduced later if needed, but just the act of selecting a colour palette initially is one less thing to think about when starting new work.

There are connections between a found object and the place it was picked up. The object evokes memories of the place, the walk, the time spent gathering, who you were with, as well as the weather conditions – light, temperature, reflections, shadows, sounds and smells. All these memories can come flooding back when looking and handling found objects, even years later. Broken objects appear fragile, vulnerable and sometimes more interesting. I am drawn to partial objects rather than the whole – the discarded scraps of familiar objects. Each carefully chosen fragment has a history of its own. Where did it come from? Was it discarded, lost or abandoned? These questions trigger the imagination as connections are made and stories emerge.

Above Collection of fragments and colour study.

Right Shelley Rhodes, *Found Fragments II*.
40 x 40cm (15¾ x 15¾in).

Found Fragments is a series inspired by discarded bits of rusty metal. The found objects were used to stimulate drawing and printing on fabric and paper, to create a series of mixed-media collages. Sections were stitched together before the final construction incorporated parts of the original source material.

Stuart Haygarth collected every man-made object that he came across while walking the coast of southern England. He gathered all kinds of common detritus, whether broken or whole. He organized and presented his collection as a series of visually beautiful photographs. The objects are carefully curated, categorized by type and colour, and precisely arranged. The pictures tell the story of pollution, our throwaway society, as well as forming an archive of fragments from people's lives.

Much of Alice Fox's work is also based on using found fragments, as she explains:

'Found objects and materials provide a tangible link to the locations I collected them from. They become a record of a place I've visited or frequent. I will often arrange and photograph the items, classifying things in terms of material, size, shape, colour: trying out possibilities and seeking out conversations between objects. I will often draw objects as a way of getting to know them, exploring shapes and tones. This time spent with a piece allows for thinking and ideas to develop about how I might work with it or respond to it creatively.'

Lime Kiln Objects is Alice's response to a group of metal objects found in a bonfire site in an old lime kiln on farmland in Cumbria. It included old aerosol cans, mattress springs and various unidentifiable burnt items, which were incorporated into the finished collection of work.

'I responded to the shapes and forms of the fragments by weaving surfaces to attach, stitching around the metal or creating tiny warps on the objects themselves and weaving directly onto them. I also wove flat shapes that I manipulated to make three-dimensional forms, mimicking the metal. These woven forms were then soaked in an oak gall dye bath (made using oak galls gathered on walks). The strong tannins in the dye bath reacted with the iron oxide of the metal items and the whole structures became stained and marked with a range of greys, browns and blacks with highlights of orange iron oxide.'

Above *Found plastic Fragments.*

Left Alice Fox, *Lime Kiln Objects.*

Lockdown Walks

Shelley Rhodes, *Lockdown Walks*.
30 x 30cm (12 x 12in).

During the pandemic in 2020 there was a sudden lockdown in the United Kingdom. Despite the mantra 'Stay at Home, Save Lives', we were encouraged to exercise. I went for a walk every day and alongside my daily sketching, I foraged and collected all kinds of small objects both natural and man-made – discarded detritus, items lost, things left behind. It made me look closely, observing and searching out little treasures that could have been overlooked. Back home I laid them out, sorting, arranging and rearranging. My growing collection was reminiscent of the school nature table, with a jumble of interesting objects, each one a reminder of my daily outing, providing a tangible link to my local area.

I placed the objects on little snippets of naturally dyed fabric and scraps of eco prints that were lying around my studio – remnants from ongoing work. This formed another connection to my local environment, as they had been dyed using leaves, berries, nettles and dandelions from my garden or picked on local walks. *Lockdown Walks* presents mundane objects, carefully curated and displayed like jewels. They have no intrinsic value but are a precious reminder of wonderful walks, my little bit of freedom whilst in lockdown.

MUSEUM COLLECTIONS

Artefacts displayed in museums can inspire new work but I am also interested in how the objects are ordered, arranged and displayed. The Pitt Rivers Museum in Oxford, England, is a favourite of mine and can be viewed online. In museums, I am intrigued by the selection, layout and position of one object next to another, as well as the space in between. I love how things are held down with pins, seemingly random numbers stamped on tags that are attached with string, or a twist of wire and labels with illegible writing that are placed amongst the objects.

Museums usually only display a very small selection from their overall collection, with many more objects stored away from public view.

  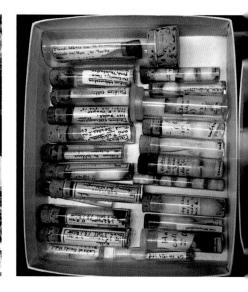

Top Archive collection, National Museums Liverpool.

Above Sketchbook page: museum annotations.

If you have a chance to look behind the scenes in the archives or snatch a glimpse of the office area, you may see index cards cataloguing the specimens, classification tickets, lists, charts and rubber stamps, boxes stacked up high and tied with string, display trays, bundles, packages and parcels.

When I visited the archives of the World Museum in Liverpool, I saw semi-transparent bags with half-hidden contents, envelopes, tickets, slide mounts, glass jars and test tubes. There were boxes within boxes: containers that were rectangular, square, round, even hexagonal, slotting together like a honeycomb. I made notes, drawings and diagrams and took photographs for later reference. Experiencing this 'behind the scenes' view was fascinating, to see not only the objects but how they are classified, stored and labelled. All of these things can be a great source of inspiration for the presentation of work (see Presenting Fragments, page 130).

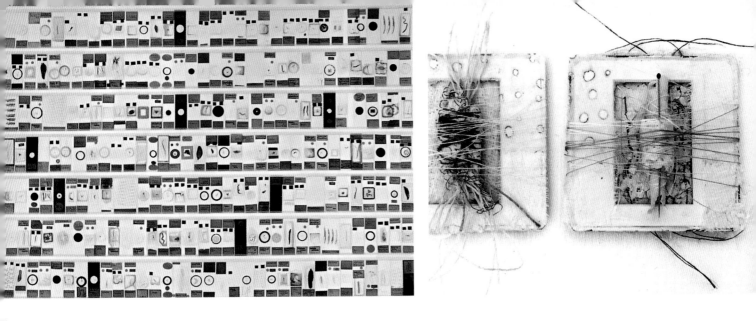

I love the use of multiples, so I was thrilled to discover the microscope slides in the Micrarium at The Grant Museum of Zoology in London. Within the museum, a small storeroom has been converted into a beautiful backlit space displaying 2,323 specimen slides and 252 lantern slides from the collection. As I walked into the space, I felt surrounded by the power of multiples. Each slide is similar but different and is like a small framed work of art, repeated and ordered in a grid format. Slide mounts can act as frames for tiny exhibits (see salvaged metal used as mini frames on page 22).

When I visit a museum, I usually make simple drawings and annotations, recording detail: I often find this more useful than drawing a whole object, as I extract shapes, pattern, texture and marks from the exhibits, my selection and editing process has already begun. In the studio, these marks inspire printing blocks, cut-outs, stencils and monoprints. The marks can be redrawn at a different scale, using a variety of mark-making tools and handmade brushes. I also use these small observational studies to inspire stitched marks.

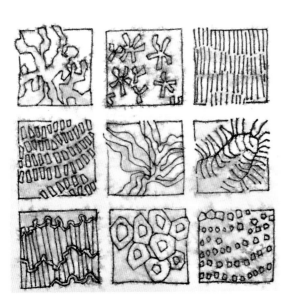

Top left Micrarium, Grant Museum of Zoology, London.

Left Sketchbook page: museum drawings.

Top Shelley Rhodes, *Specimen Case* (detail).

Above Decorated papers.

Shelley Rhodes, *The Fragile Remains*.
Part of an installation inspired
by museum displays.

The Fragile Remains

The presentation of museum collections inspired work with the overall title of *The Fragile Remains*, which comprises of many carefully curated objects, fragments, models, tiny handmade books, bundles, rolls and stacks, presented within boxes, trays and frames. Each piece can be presented individually or as an installation of multiple pieces, depending on the space in which they are to be displayed.

During my research into coral bleaching and rising sea temperatures, I discovered that coral reefs are also affected by discarded plastic. Plastic bags and fishing line can become entangled and wrapped around the delicate coral, causing damage. With this in mind, I gathered discarded plastic while beachcombing. Some of it reminded me of marine life –

squashed plastic bottles resembling jelly fish, bottle tops like crustaceans wrapped with tendril-like fishing line. I transformed the salvaged plastic into delicate 'sea creatures', presenting them alongside natural objects, inviting the viewer to look closely in order to distinguish the real from the man-made. They are labelled, entangled and cocooned with plastic I gathered from beaches, and displayed in boxes and cases as though they are exquisite, extinct specimens (see *Specimen Drawer*, page 125 and *Specimen Case*, page 127).

I want the viewer to ask, what does the future hold if we do not stop littering our coast with damaging plastic debris? Will the only coral that our descendants see be the fragile remains in museums?

DISPLAYING FRAGMENTS

People have collected objects and found pleasure in displaying them for centuries. In the sixteenth century, 'cabinets of curiosities' became popular, as aristocrats displayed notable collections of objects, although these were usually presented in a special room rather than being displayed in a cabinet. In effect, these were the precursors to museums. All kinds of eclectic objects could be displayed, including religious and historic relics, works of art and archaeological fragments. Natural history objects were commonly featured, particularly rare shells, corals, fossils, skeletons and insects.

Above Shelley Rhodes, *Boxes within Boxes*. Work in progress.

Placing an item – or even a tiny fragment – within a box can elevate it to greater importance, inviting closer inspection, making it seem cherished and special. Filling frames, boxes, cases and drawers is a way of creating order, as fragments and relics are carefully fitted into selected spaces. There are often connections between the items but sometimes an unrelated object will jolt the viewer and grab their attention. This type of selection, categorization and presentation is something that filters into many artists' work. Mark Dion often collaborates with museums, scientists and members of the public to excavate, collect, order and display objects. His interest lies in what we select to conserve, what we choose to cherish or to discard.

Below Shelley Rhodes, *Specimen Case* (details).

Discarded plastic

I gathered abandoned plastic sacks found on beaches that had been weathered and worn by the sea. Some were marked with rusty stains, others had rips, holes and ragged edges. Some felt like cloth: they had been pummelled by the ocean, yet they were not disintegrating. Carefully observing the sacks, I made a series of large drawings, some on paper and some on cloth. I made drawing tools from the sacks and used them to draw with ink. The drawings were fragmented to make a series of mixed-media pieces incorporating the plastic sacking. I also stitched into the plastic sacks, treating them like fabric, adding fragments of weathered cloth and stitched marks inspired by my drawing. I pulled strands from plastic rope and the edges of the plastic sacks to use as thread. This was reminiscent of the withdrawal of threads from the edges of the worn saris used in kantha making.

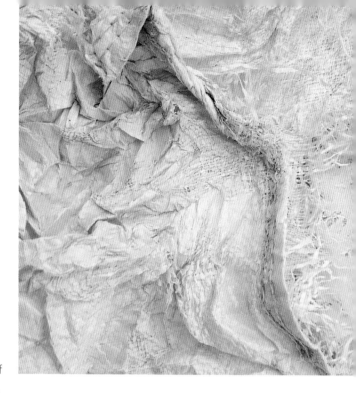

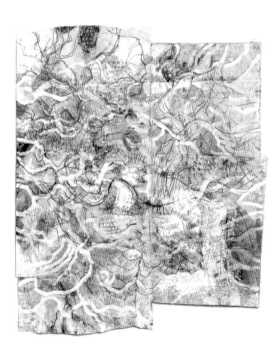

Similarly, Siân Martin became increasingly aware of the polluting effect of discarded plastic that often ends up in the sea. She gathered plastic bottles from beaches and fragmented these into smaller pieces, so she could investigate the idea of mending, repairing and healing, as she explains:

'I began to transform the bottles by sanding down the shiny, plastic surface so they became matt. Then I cut them into numerous pieces, which allowed me to explore ways of stitching and re-joining. I'm intrigued by ways of suggesting the idea of "change", forming a gradual movement from one state to another by adding, subtracting, modifying sizes, adjusting and intensifying colour.'

Top Plastic collection.

Above left Shelley Rhodes, *Plastic Sack Drawing*. 83 x 70cm (32½ x 27½in).

Above right Shelley Rhodes, *Stitched Plastic*. Work in progress.

Siân felt the process of breaking, dissolving and disintegrating could also be applied to the breakdown of the ecological system.

'I melted rows of small holes enabling me to thread or lace segments together – mending to make perfect, although in reality distorted versions of the original. Twisted, fragmented shapes, sanded and scratched – using only portions of a whole bottle to suggest a sense of disintegration or gradual disappearance.'

Above Shelley Rhodes,
White Plastic Bundles.
30 x 30cm
(12 x 12in).

Below Siân Martin,
*Fragmented Plastic
Bottles.*

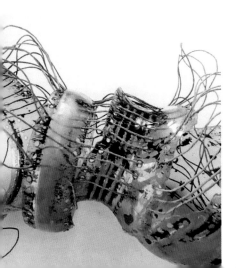

CONTAINERS

Vessels, containers and boxes offer a form of protection, often making the items inside seem precious. I am reminded of the small shrines known as *kandylakia*, seen on roadsides in Greece, in which personal objects, candles and icons are carefully placed and protected within their container, adding gravitas. They mark lives lost but also lives spared.

Debbie Lyddon often makes containers in her work, and these have a particular significance, as she explains:

'I think of each one as a holding place. I like the wordplay this describes. The container can be either for holding a sense of place, where materials and processes define the environment I am evoking; or the container literally holds place as I put found objects inside it.'

Enclosed: Exposed is an example of a 'holding place' in both senses of her definition and encompasses ideas of protection.

'The work demonstrates a snapshot of time and explores the effect that natural processes have on a shifting, dynamic coastline – a place of transience and uncertainty. Two containers hold a series of tightly packed, small pots. The first series considers how, when exposed to the effects of the weather, objects become unstable and will eventually break down. Whilst the second series suggests that, when protected, objects can be robust and stand up to the elements.'

The arrangement and placement of the objects is important. The space between objects can be regular or irregular, close together or far apart, as Debbie elaborates:

'I move objects around, adding and taking away until I have an arrangement that gives what artist Sandra Blow called "that startling rightness". The groupings form small landscapes that suggest a sense of time, space, mood or atmosphere.'

Top *Kandylakia*, Greece.

Left Debbie Lyddon, *Exposed: Enclosed.* 7 x 25 x 20cm (2¾ x 9¾ x 8in).

BOXES

American artist Joseph Cornell made several series of small-scale box constructions, which were effectively three-dimensional collages. He pasted papers, photographs and ephemera inside boxes before assembling groups of carefully selected, cast-off and discarded artefacts within them. The boxes were usually wood with a sealed glass pane. He would seek out bric-a-brac and was fascinated by fragments of once beautiful and precious objects. He enclosed one thing inside another – placing the objects within drawers, frames, compartments, boxes and on shelves – creating a compact version of a cabinet of curiosity.

On a larger scale, contemporary artist Leonardo Drew uses hundreds of closely packed rust-encrusted boxes, filled with rags and debris, to reference and symbolize the terrible living conditions of slaves. He uses processes of oxidation, burning and decay to create huge installations that are dramatic, powerful and mesmerizing.

My *Specimen Drawer* has individual compartments. The sections contain 'specimens', made mostly from plastic detritus combined with tiny, natural fragments found on the beach – small assemblages to represent extinct sea creatures. They were constructed using a combination of salvaged plastic, paper pulp, fabric, thread, paper, wire and paper porcelain clay. The position of one item next to another is important. Consideration was given to the overall balance of the piece, as I opted to leave some spaces, alluding to the loss of species. The lack of colour represents bleached coral and its further demise by disease and entanglement caused by discarded plastic.

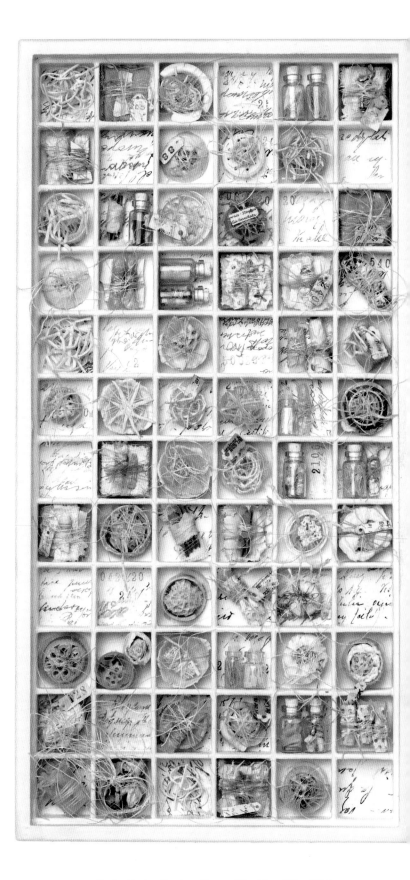

Shelley Rhodes, *Specimen Drawer*. 25 x 48cm (9¾ x 19in).

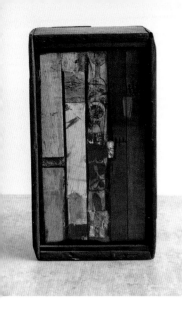  

Fragments in boxes

Hannelore Baron made box constructions from damaged, salvaged wood and metal. These were sometimes tied with string or nailed together. They contain fragments of paper and cloth, some presented as rolls and scrolls, or wrapped and bound into bundles, then placed in little compartments. They are intriguing and mysterious with hidden secrets and half-concealed objects. These small works made from repurposed materials draw you in. There is an intimacy, vulnerability and fragility to the work. Having escaped the horrors of the Holocaust in 1941, Hannelore uses the various discarded materials tenderly, as though they have survived and been given a second chance of a new life.

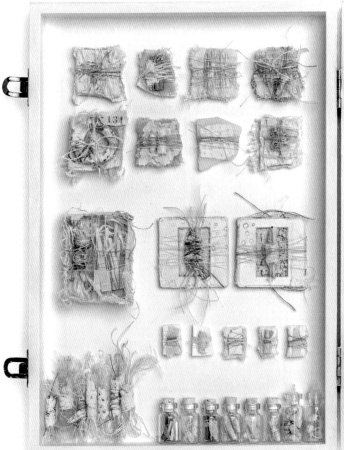
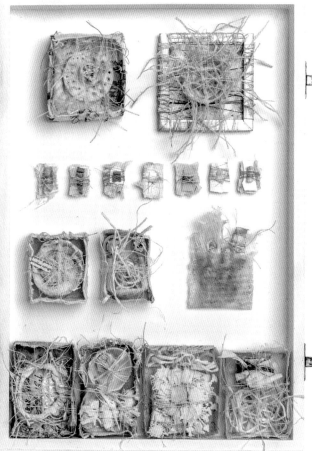

Above Shelley Rhodes,
Specimen Case.
32 x 45cm
(12½ x 17¾in).

In *Specimen Case*, I display boxes within boxes as I emulate a display of museum artefacts. Boxes were made from a variety of materials, such as painted calico, muslin stiffened with clear matt varnish, and stitched fabric coated with plaster and paint (see Materials, page 136). Some were made from paper that had been drawn and printed on prior to construction. Glue, stitch and tape hold the boxes together. Specimens were made using fragments of discarded plastic gathered from beaches. Alongside the boxes, some are presented as stacks or bundles, others on slide mounts or in test tubes. A great deal of consideration was given to the arrangement of the objects. The specimens were placed in groups. I looked, I contemplated, then I moved them; I left them, then I came back, I looked again, and then moved them again. Things were added, others were taken away. Sometimes I photographed the arrangement. It was an ongoing process until finally the whole piece felt balanced.

Opposite, top left Hannelore Baron (1926–1987),
Untitled (B81060), 1981, box assemblage of wood, glass,
ink, paper, fabric and monoprint. 30 x 17 x 9cm
(12 x 6¾ x 3⅝in), signed.

Opposite, top centre Hannelore Baron (1926–1987),
Untitled (B84054), 1984, box assemblage of wood, fabric,
ink, paint and monoprint. 26 x 17.5 x 7cm
(10 x 7 x 2¾in), signed.

Opposite, top right Hannelore Baron (1926–1987),
Untitled (B85041), 1985, box assemblage with wood,
paint and nails. 22 x 21 x 5cm (8⅝ x 8⅜ x 2in), signed.

Opposite, top left Hannelore Baron (1926–1987),
Untitled (B82028), 1982, painted metal box assemblage
with metal, monotype and ink. 11 x 14 x 4.5cm
(4½ x 5⅝ x 1¾in), signed.

All images © Estate of Hannelore Baron; Courtesy
of Michael Rosenfeld Gallery LLC, New York, NY.

Deconstructed boxes

Boxes do not have to remain whole. Cardboard boxes can be flattened or dismantled to create a surface for painting or for using as collage – it's great to make use of free packaging by recycling and reusing. They can be manipulated, fragmented, squashed and stitched to create an imperfect box. Tears or irregularities can be repaired with decorative stitches, wire, staples or pins.

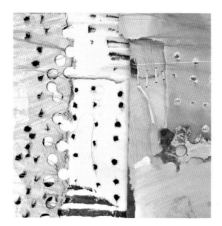

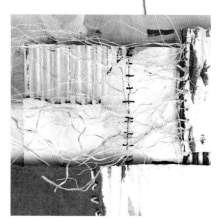

Elizabeth Couzins-Scott uses fragmented boxes as a form of containment in which to place her fragile assemblages. The work, in the form of an installation, is concerned with the degradation of the oceans. She displays a series of artefacts that represent the remains of lost sea life – presented as a reliquary, incorporating remnants and traces of materials.

'I have adopted an intuitive and flexible approach in response to materials. I am interested in recycling and the transformation of found materials, which I combine with handmade paper, cloth, stitch, wire and thread to make assemblages from disparate components – allowing a heterogeneity of media to explain the idea. I collect all kinds of materials to embed in paper pulp – items collected from the seashore: plant materials, broken shells, bones, seed pods and scraps of metal. Pulp is easily manipulated when wet, enabling textured surfaces to be created by moulding, casting and layering. Gesso or paint can be added to create heavily textured impasto surfaces, which can be impressed with tools, scratched or cracked. When dry, they can be sanded and painted to make a strong, light form.'

Top Shelley Rhodes, *Recycled Box Collage.* 15 x 15cm (6 x 6in).

Above Deconstructed box assemblages (details).

Elizabeth considered how to present these intricate and delicate forms for a long time before realizing that any box or container in which they were placed also had to be distressed, imperfect and not quite whole. So, she created a specific environment for each piece, which became as important as the assemblage contained within it.

Elizabeth Couzins-Scott,
Fragmented Box Reliquaries.
Approx. 13 x 13cm (5 x 5in) each.

PRESENTING FRAGMENTS

The way something is presented and displayed interests me – attention to detail, arrangement and layout relates to my training in graphic design. Hideyuki Oka wrote a series of books about traditional Japanese packaging that demonstrate how very ordinary, humble things can be presented in beautiful ways. Taking care to present even the most inconsequential ephemeral objects in an aesthetically pleasing way gives them greater importance and invites the viewer to look closer.

Museums can be a great source of inspiration (see Museum Collections, page 118). Investigate, explore and consider ways to present fragments – on labels, in envelopes or on index cards, for example. Objects may be contained within small bags or pockets, which could be semi-transparent, made from glassine, tracing paper or silk organza.

Fragments can be displayed three-dimensionally by using them to create models, bundles, rolls and stacks, or they may be displayed in jars, test tubes or glass vials.

Above and opposite, above
Presenting fragments (details).

Below Sketchbook sample page.

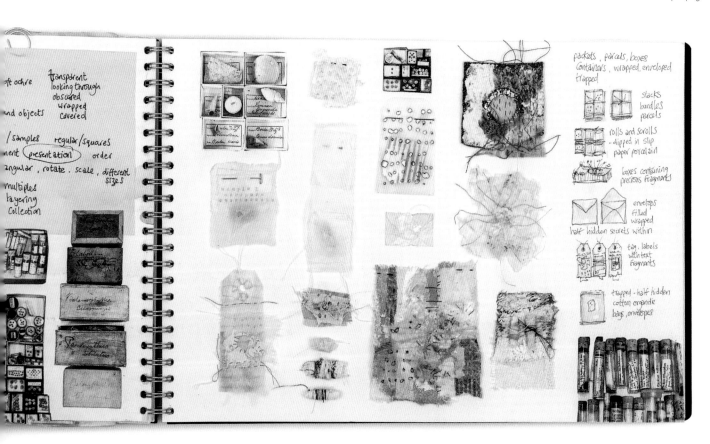

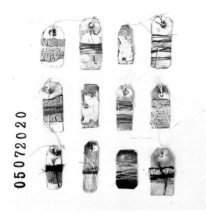

Gillian Lowndes trained as a ceramic artist but increasingly incorporated fragments and found objects into her three-dimensional work. Her mixed-media assemblages include discarded man-made objects, such as crockery, bulldog clips and cloth, as well as natural materials like shells, loofahs, horsehair and dried plant roots. She took an experimental approach and claimed that the materials and process produced the ideas, not the other way around. She combined disparate objects with latex, fibreglass and clay before firing them in the kiln, then gluing or stitching them together with wire.

Below Shelley Rhodes, *Stacks.*
4 x 5 x 7cm (1½ x 2 x 2¾in) each.

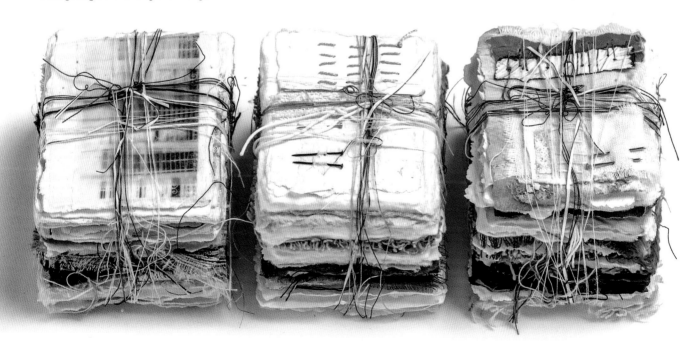

MIXED MEDIA

Mixed-media art combines more than one type of media or material in a single artwork. This usually involves layering, but really there are no rules. This can lead to experimentation and artistic play. Ask yourself 'What will happen if …?', then have a go to find out.

'Take an object. Do something to it. Do something else to it.'

Jasper Johns

LAYERING

I often explore materials and media not always associated with textiles. I alter the surface of cloth and paper by applying plaster, paint, pigments, clay slip, wax, varnish and chalk, or combinations of these materials. For the plaster mix, I combine emulsion paint or gesso with a similar amount of water, then add a few spoons of builder's plaster. Once dry, the surface can be manipulated by cracking, folding and creasing. Clay slip is made by adding water to clay, leaving it to soften, and then mixing it to the consistency of double cream. This can be applied to fabric and when dry the coated surfaces can be scratched,

torn and repaired, or fragmented then joined. I tend to use porcelain clay or porcelain paper clay, which has the addition of paper fibres, but any clay can be used. With both of these methods, if washes of ink and paint are applied, they run into the cracks and crevices, enhancing the texture. If they are too flaky or delicate, clear matt varnish can be used to seal them. Colour can be introduced by rubbing soft chalks or pigments onto the surface. Rubbing in a little boiled linseed oil on a rag moves the pigment around, adding a slight sheen and sealing the surface. Safety note: always wear a mask when mixing powders, rubbing or sanding.

Shelley Rhodes, *Specimen Cards* (details).

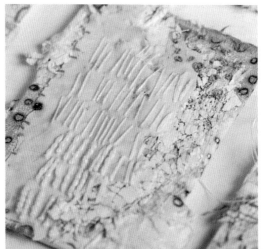

Above Experimental mixed-media sample.

Left Mixed media with stitch: work in progress.

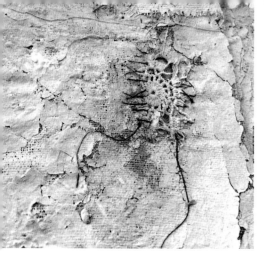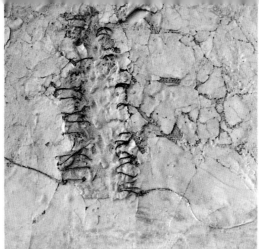

I build the work up in layers. For example, I may piece and patch fabric first – joining with stitch, perhaps creating folds and tucks; then, when the paint and plaster mix is applied, the stitches become embedded.

The order of application and different strengths of mix will give different results. There are no real rules – by experimenting and exploring you may discover some exciting combinations that can be used in your mixed-media and textile work. Here are a few suggestions to get you started.

Things to try

1. Stitch the fabric first, then apply the media.
2. Apply various media to samples in different orders to see if they react differently.
3. Stitch rusty objects to fabric before embedding with media, then allow to weather.
4. Manipulate, crack and crease the fabric once it is dry.
5. Apply colour with washes of paint and ink, or rub in chalk and pigments with a little boiled linseed oil.

Above Mixed media (details).

Below Shelley Rhodes, *Backstreets Series* (details).

Specimen Cards is a series mounted on small canvas boards, part of a larger group of work in which I have explored damage to coral reefs. The work captures the fragility of the coral when it loses its colour and becomes brittle, cracked and broken. It is presented as individual units referencing a museum cataloguing system. Plaster, porcelain slip and paint were applied to various types of cloth that were manipulated once dry to form cracks. These were then joined and 'repaired' before being reassembled onto the boards using acrylic matt gel, and clear matt varnish was used to seal areas that were particularly flaky.

Above Shelley Rhodes, *Specimen Cards.* 9.5 x 7cm (3¾ x 2¾in) each.

MATERIALS

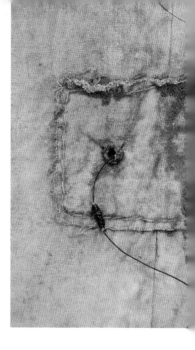

Debbie Lyddon often coats cloth in various protective substances before subjecting it to further weathering and staining processes. She lives in north Norfolk on the east coast of England, where she observes the use of maritime cloth, alluding to its functional use in much of her work, as she explains:

'Tarpaulins and boat covers are protective cloths but in order to do their job properly they, in turn, need to be protected from the effects of the weather. The materials with which I coat the cloth – wax, linseed oil, bitumen and paint – are substances that have been traditionally used to preserve and protect sails, ropes and nets, and the dressing of my work with these materials plays an integral part in relating the cloth objects I make to the people and landscape of the coast.'

She considers the effect the sea and the weather have on cloth and the processes of change that occur when it is exposed to the elements. She is interested in both the process of protecting cloth from the elements, and the degeneration and disintegration of cloth that has been unprotected:

'I explore the effects the elements themselves have on cloth and how it can mark it. I like to use materials readily available to me and seawater is outside my studio door in abundance. I sew iron wire eyelets and other found rusty objects into the work I make, and throw them into the sea so that the iron will rust and mark the cloth – rusting is a process that is happening continuously in the environment around me.

Salt, contained in seawater, has also become a significant material and is central to my exploration of how the environment and weather processes can affect and alter cloth. Inspired by the salt rime that stains sea-soaked cloth and the dry salt crust that forms on salt marshes, salt is a material that not only connects my work directly to the local coastal landscape, but it also describes processes of change over time.'

Debbie Lyddon, mixed-media work including hand-ground pigments – chalk and yellow ochre – bitumen, wax, metal, salt, seawater, rust and natural staining.

USING EVERY LAST SCRAP

I keep the smallest scraps, offcuts and leftover bits from whatever I am working on, whether it is drawing, printmaking, collage or stitched work. The tiny fragments left after trimming or tearing are stored in small ziplock bags. These fragments are used as layers in sketchbooks, for collage, or they may become the start of new work.

MOTTAINAI

The Japanese word *mottainai* translates as 'too good to waste', in other words to use every last scrap and remnant – taking the idea of recycling and reusing to the extreme. When painting and printing, I place a piece of paper or fabric on my work surface to protect it; the random marks, drips, splatters and stains can be beautiful, and I often reuse these pieces within my work. Paper and fabric scraps are all kept. At the end of one particular project, the pieces became smaller and smaller. I used them to make tiny little compositions – joining, stitching and wrapping, then taking pleasure in arranging and positioning the multiple jewel-like pieces to make *Fragments x48*.

Right Shelley Rhodes,
Fragments x48.
30 x 30cm (12 x 12in).

Below right Shelley
Rhodes, *Recycled Print.*
17 x 17cm
(6¾ x 6¾in).

Keep everything

During my workshops I advise students not
to discard or throw away drawings or prints
they consider do not work, as often within a
discarded piece, there will be small
areas that look stunning when isolated.
I once rescued a student's print from the
bin at the end of the day – it was slightly
smudged and unevenly printed, so had been
discarded. Selecting areas from it using a
small viewfinder, I cut and rearranged the
pieces, adding a little bit of stitch and thread
to create a new composition. I showed the
reworked 'new work' next morning and no
one recognized the print as their own.

Opposite Shelley Rhodes, *Offcuts* (detail).

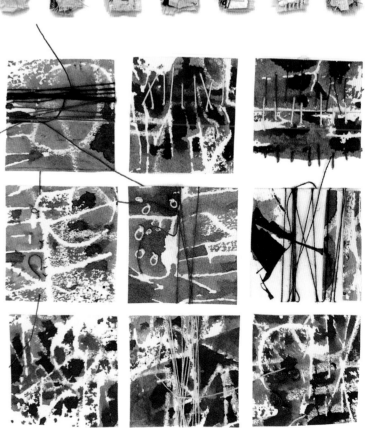

A DAILY PRACTICE

In January 2019 I started a daily stitching practice, my only rule to stitch for at least 15 minutes every day of the coming year using leftover scraps. It began as a New Year's resolution – a promise to myself to find time to stitch daily. I knew it was important to set an achievable goal, having worked every day in sketchbooks for many years. It became a habit: a repetitive but pleasurable task. Stitching with no predetermined result or plan was liberating. I used it to try things out, using leftover bits usually discarded.

I cut a 1m (3¼ft) strip of soft cotton to use as a base fabric, then gradually secured fragments, pinning initially before stitching down. I did not have a specific plan but let the piece grow organically. When I finished stitching the first strip, I joined a second. Stitching in 1m sections, then joining them, made each section portable and easy to take with me when travelling so that I could continue with my 15 minutes each day.

I used the practice as a stitch sampler to explore and test stitched marks that were loosely linked to my ongoing work investigating coral, and many of the scraps were offcuts from the project. The stitched marks were often interpretations of the marks and patterns observed on coral fragments. Other stitches were experimental. I pieced and patched, distressed and repaired, using *boro* textiles as inspiration. I showed it in workshops, to demonstrate stitches and methods of layering fragments, but I never intended to exhibit it as a finished piece of work. By the time I had completed my year of daily stitching, there was something special about the way the piece draped and folded, enabling different areas to be seen next to each other. It grew little by little and turned into something quite beautiful.

Below Shelley Rhodes, *Little By Little*.
13 x 750cm (5 x 295in).
Details shown opposite.

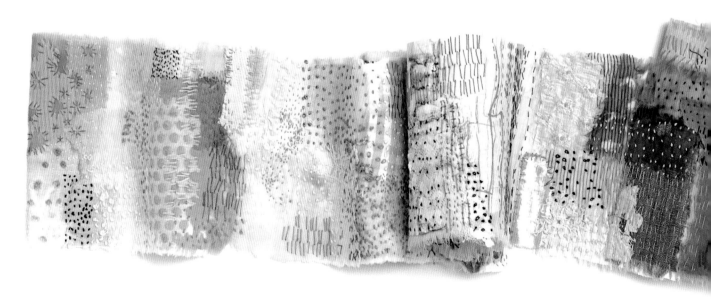

FINAL THOUGHTS

Do not discard things that are fragmented or seemingly mundane, as they can provide inspiration for drawing and mark-making and may be included in finished work. Looking closely and embracing imperfection can lead to stimulating and visually exciting work. Allow traditional methods of repair to inspire and stimulate innovative, contemporary ways to join and reassemble. Finally, remember that everything can be altered and adjusted – if something is not working, it can be reworked, and often the results will be far more dynamic and exciting than the original.

'There is only one way to learn. It's through action. Everything you need to know you have learned through your journey.'

Paulo Coelho

CONTRIBUTING ARTISTS

I am very grateful to all the artists who have made an invaluable contribution to this book:

Beverly Ayling-Smith	www.beverlyaylingsmith.com
Sharon Brown	www.instagram.com/sharonjbrownartist
Jenny Bullen	www.textilestudygroup.co.uk/members/jenny-bullen/
Elizabeth Couzins-Scott	www.axisweb.org/p/elizabethcouzinsscott/
Alice Fox	www.alicefox.co.uk
Matthew Harris	www.matthewharriscloth.co.uk
Debbie Lyddon	www.debbielyddon.co.uk
Siân Martin	www.distantstitch.co.uk
Jan Miller	www.62group.org.uk/artist/jan-miller/
Sally Payne	www.instagram.com/sallysladepayne
Wen Redmond	www.wenredmond.com
Dorothy Tucker	www.textilestudygroup.co.uk/members/dorothy-tucker/
Donna Watson	www.donnawatsonart.com
Thanks to **Jim Austin**	www.kimonoboy.com

Author: Shelley Rhodes www.shelleyrhodes.co.uk www.instagram.com/shelleyrhodesartist
www.facebook.com/shelleyrhodesmixedmediaartist

Shelley Rhodes, *Coral Cloth*. 115 x 37cm (45¼ x 14½in).

FURTHER READING

Barker, Emma, *Contemporary Cultures of Display* (Yale University Press, 1999)

Gallery Kei & Sri, *Mottainai: The Fabric of Life* (Exhibition catalogue, 2011)

Gillow, John and Pratapaditya Pal, *Kantha: Recycled and Embroidered Textiles of Bengal* (Radius, 2017)

Glaser, Jessica and Susan Kruse, *Bringing Back the Book: How the Library of Lost Books Explores the Creative Potential of Discarded Books* (Library of Lost Books, 2013)

Gostelow, Mary, *Embroidery: Traditional Designs, Techniques and Patterns from All Over the World* (Marshall Cavendish, 1977)

Haygarth, Stuart, *Strand* (Art Books Publishing, 2016)

Husain, Surjeet, *Kantha Embroidery: A Workbook* (Unknown publisher, 2008)

Koide, Yukiko and Kyoichi Tsuzuki, *Boro: Rags and Tatters from the Far North of Japan* (Aspect Corp., 2009)

Koren, Leonard, *Wabi-sabi: For Artists, Designers, Poets & Philosophers* (Imperfect Publishing, 2008)

Longhurst, Erin Niimi, *Japonisme: Ikigai, Forest Bathing, Wabi-sabi and More* (Harper Thorsons, 2018)

Mauriès, Patrick, *Cabinets of Curiosities* (Thames and Hudson, 2011)

Noguchi, Hikaru, *Darning: Repair, Make, Mend* (Hawthorn Press, 2019)

Oka, Hideyuki, *How to Wrap Five More Eggs* (Weatherhill, Inc., 2008)

Paine, Sheila, *Embroidered Textiles* (Thames and Hudson, 2010)

Plowman, Randel, *Masters: Collage* (Lark Books, 2010)

Putman, James, *Art and Artifact: The Museum as Medium* (Thames and Hudson, 2001)

Redmond, Wen, *Digital Fiber Art* (C&T Publishing, 2016)

Styles, John, *Threads of Feeling: The London Foundling Hospital's Textile Tokens 1740–1770* (The Foundling Museum, 2010)

Waldman, Diane, *Joseph Cornell: Master of Dreams* (Abrams, 2006)

ACKNOWLEDGEMENTS

I would like to thank all the talented artists who have contributed by generously giving their time and sharing their work, as well as the museums and galleries for allowing me to show images. A huge thank you to everyone at Batsford, in particular my editor Nicola Newman.

I would like to thank my husband Bryan for his help with proofreading, as well as his never-ending love and support, and as always love and thanks to my mum Thelma Thomas for always encouraging and believing in me.

Photographs by Michael Wicks and Shelley Rhodes except the following: 7 William Phillip, reproduced with kind permission of the Embroiderers' Guild; 12, 13, 14 (top) Jim Austin at www.kimonoboy.com; 29 (bottom), 36, 124 (bottom), 136–137 Debbie Lyddon; 34, 35 (top), 116 (bottom) Carolyn Mendelsohn; 45 (left), 130 (bottom) Electric Egg; 54 (all images), 109 (bottom) Article Studio; 55 Matthew Harris; 56, 57 (top) Joao Pedro; 57 (bottom) Richard Brayshaw; 58 © Coram (www.coram.org.uk); 60–61 Sharon Brown; 64, 65, 123 (bottom) Siân Martin; 65 (right) Kevin Mead; 68, 69 Wen Redmond; 80 (middle) Jan Miller; 81 (all images) Eleanor Torbati; 96, 97 (bottom) Sally Payne; 104 Alice Fox; 105 Beverly Ayling-Smith; 107, 126 (all images) © Estate of Hannelore Baron, Courtesy of Michael Rosenfeld Gallery LLC, New York, NY; 108, 109 (top) Donna Watson; 118 (top) images reproduced with kind permission of National Museums Liverpool; 119 (top left) with thanks to the Grant Museum of Zoology, UCL.

INDEX